Upland
Stream

Books by W. D. Wetherell

Souvenirs
Vermont River
The Man Who Loved Levittown
Hyannis Boat and Other Stories
Chekhov's Sister
Upland Stream

Upland
Stream

Notes on the Fishing Passion

W. D. WETHERELL

LITTLE, BROWN AND COMPANY

BOSTON   NEW YORK   TORONTO   LONDON

First Paperback Edition

Illustrations by Michael McCurdy

Grateful acknowledgment is made to the following publications in which some of these pieces were first published: *Reader's Digest, Vermont Life, New England Monthly, The Fly-Fisher, Broadside, Fly-Fishing Heritage,* and *Seasons of the Angler.*

The author wishes to thank Robert Traver for permission to reprint "Testament of a Fisherman."

Library of Congress Cataloging-in-Publication Data
Wetherell, W. D.
      Upland Stream : notes on the fishing passion /
W. D. Wetherell — 1st ed.
          p.   cm.
      1. Fishing.   2. Fishing stories.   I. Title.
SH441.W48 — 1991
799.1 — dc20   90-24750
      ISBN 0-316-93175-6

10   9   8   7   6   5   4   3

MV-NY

*Published simultaneously in Canada
by Little, Brown & Company (Canada) Limited*

Printed in the United States of America

For
Matthew David Wetherell, *born May 23, 1990,*
and in memory of
Walter Davidson Wetherell, *born May 23, 1887*

Contents

Upland
Stream

January 16

I have this weakness as an essay writer: when I start out with the intention of writing an essay about, say, middle age, the subject has a way of swerving around toward fly-fishing; when I sit down to write an essay about fly-fishing, it hops tracks and ends up being about middle age. My solution in this book is to let these tendencies have their head, and my own purpose here at the start is to warn fly-fishers and nonfishers that the swerves may not always go in the direction they would wish.

There's another thing to remember: I write fiction for a living — my job is to lie as persuasively as I can. Link this to the natural tendency of a fisherman to exaggerate and embellish and there may be a passage or two where even the most patient credulity is strained. Nevertheless, except for the parts where I very broadly wink, and a few protective pseudonyms, the events in this book are true, and the only liberty I've taken is to sometimes rearrange their chronology, the better to bring everything into the yearly focus on which the essays are framed. Here in rural New England the seasonal cycle is the adventure by which we all live, and a fisherman's slice of it is made richer by its fleeting and bittersweet briefness. I don't think I'm to be blamed for wanting to slow the clock down from time to time, stop the hands from moving faster, and even occasionally push them back.

Mid-January now — a good time to be thinking of streams and rivers and trout. A good time, too, to pay tribute to the man who got me started writing about fishing, the editor and essayist who has written and published more good fishing in print than anyone in the literature of our sport, Nick Lyons.

Twenty-three below zero last night by the thermometer on our porch, and yet there are barrel-sized openings in the ice, and from their centers the river draws its breath in frosty puffs, gearing up now for spring.

Upland Stream

There can't be too many places in the world where it's possible to stand in all four seasons simultaneously and be uncomfortable in each. The hills above my home are one of them — the oddly beautiful, oddly tortured New Hampshire hills of granite and spruce, brook trout and beaver, bogwater and Frost. By late April the snow is almost gone there, though enough remains to trap, squeeze, and soak heavy boots. The leaves, last autumn's crop of them, lie in slick matted heaps on the forest floor, their red and gold blended into an amber in-betweenness with the treacherous texture of mud. The sun, with no shade on the trees, burns even faster than in July. The wind, the thawing vernal wind, slaps back and forth like a wet towel, adding a chill in your middle to go along with the chill in your toes. Add a few precocious blackflies, potholes of slush, and some fresh tangled blowdowns and you have a pretty thorough set of variations on one masochistic theme. Come spring and the start of the trout season I would be nowhere else.

It's Copper Run I'm talking about here, the small upland stream I've come to love in the course of five years' fishing. Never wider than ten feet, never deeper than four, it drains a small unspoiled corner of New England woods, leaching as it does so all the beauty to be found there, so that it becomes the liquid, flowing locus of the surrounding hills. Seldom visited, it's possible to walk along the banks the better part of a day without coming upon any human trace other than a rusty bolt or tinny water can dropped by a logger fifty years before. Not in every pool but enough to make it interesting there are trout — miniature brook trout that seem in their color and quickness to be essence of stream, spontaneously generated, living crystals of orange and black. To take even a single six-incher — for one short moment to be attached to something so vivid and alive — is reason enough to suffer the multiple discomforts of the April woods.

There are more mundane reasons, of course. The need once the weather warms to bolt from the prison a house can become. The need to justify the new graphite rod I treated myself to at Christmas. The need after a long winter's writing to be out and questing after something besides words. Around the third week in April these things reach their peak, and it only takes a gentle, triggerlike pressure — a surge of sunlight? geese returning? a southerly cast to the wind? — to make me shed the last of my inertia and make the five-mile migration that separates a Copper Run longed for and imagined from a Copper Run stood beside and real.

Last April's trip could stand for any. There was the busy rummaging in the closet for leaders and flies, the casual "Think I'll try a few casts up on the mountain" to a knowing

Celeste, the raid on the refrigerator for nuts and oranges, the hydroplaning, swerving ride up our dirt road that in mud season passes for driving — the abrupt dead-end when the ruts became frozen and the joyride stopped.

The stopping point varies each year, but I'm usually left with an uphill walk of at least a mile. On this trip it was a little more than that; I made it to the frozen pond where the deep woods begin, parked on an icy pull-off, pushed my rod into a rucksack, and started off on foot. It had been a hard winter, and the earth in the middle of the road was still in the process of turning itself over, lined with the stiff petrified creases that are, I suppose, the earthy equivalents of groans. There by the marge the ground was softer, potted with moose prints. I've seen moose here in the past on their journeys from pond to pond — great lumbering browns wearing a look of perpetual bafflement, as if they can't quite figure out who or what they are or whether they should care.

At about the same time the hardwood starts giving way to spruce there comes a perceptible flattening as you emerge on the height of land. There's a bridge here, nothing more than a rude corduroy, and it's possible to walk right across it without realizing a trickle of water flows beneath. Leave the road — follow the trickle through the first tangled briars — and in less than twenty yards you come to the start of Copper Run proper at the towering Gateway Arch.

I call it this quite deliberately for the drama of the May evening I discovered it. Celeste was pregnant, and in the course of one of our evening walks for exercise we crossed the corduroy bridge on our way to a small pond whose star attraction, besides its wildness, was a resident loon. I had my rod with me, of course; I caught perch in the pond's shallows as Celeste readied our picnic and poured out our tea. After dinner, curious, I left her admiring the sunset while I walked back to the bridge and followed the trickle upstream to see if I couldn't find where it began.

It began in a beaver pond, as it turned out, and a big one; on the far shore, framed by the fingers of dying tree trunks, rose the gray bulk of Slide Mountain, emphasizing the vastness even more. There were insects hatching everywhere; between their rings, the wake left by the resident beaver, and a slight evening wind, the surface of the pond buzzed with as much activity as Lake Sunapee on a weekend afternoon. I managed to balance along the beaver dam to a place I could cast, but if there were trout in the pond they were occupied elsewhere and I soon gave up.

So back to the bridge then. Back to it — and then off into the woods downstream. I'm not sure what prompted me to do it; it was close to dark and the stream was more shreds and tatters than a definite flow. But the future has a magnetism all its own, and there in the twilight, in the mountain stillness, with the sensitivity toward omens even a vicarious pregnancy brings, I was more attuned to it than usual, and it would have taken a deliberate act of violence not to have given in to its pull.

"Just a little way," I told myself — the old indisputable justification. There by the bridge the bank was all briars, and it was hard enough to make any way. Since the future not only tugs us but shapes us into the correct posture to meet it, I was bowing my way (a low, reverential bow) through a particularly bad tangle when the watery tatters suddenly gathered themselves and changed from a pedestrian pewter to a rich, luminous copper; the effect was that of stepping into a sunset turned molten. At the same time, or perhaps a split second earlier, I noticed a darkening overhead, and looked up to see the branches of two white pines meet high above the stream, forming with their intersection a perfect proscenium or arch.

A Gateway Arch — the expression came to me the moment I saw it. It wasn't just the perfection of the framing, the changing color, but how both came embellished with a roll of drums — with a deepening and staccato-like increase in what had been until that moment nothing more than a vacant gurgling. Just past the arch, where color and sound were richest, was a small pool formed by the junction of two smaller streams — the outlets of the two ponds already mentioned. Waving my rod ahead of me like a Geiger counter — like the antenna of a probing ant — I shook my Muddler down into the pool's center, letting it sink toward the sharp rocks that lined its sides. Immediately there came a pull, and then a moment later a six-inch brook trout was splashing across my boots, sending up a little shiver of happiness toward my neck. I let him go, then tried another cast, this time a little farther downstream. Again, a six-inch trout, this one even deeper-bodied and more brilliantly speckled, with a soft coppery cast on his back that seemed the water's undertone.

I caught six trout in all that first evening, each a yard or so downstream of its predecessor. In the twilight, in my twilight mood, it was clear they were deliberately tugging me deeper into the woods, the better to ensnare me in their enchantment. After the sixth I broke away and waded back through the darkness toward the bridge. By the time I rejoined a worried Celeste (who knew my Hansel-like

susceptibilities well enough), the experience had settled just
far enough for me to realize I had stumbled upon what in
flinty New England terms was a virtual Shangri-la.

Something of this surprise, something of this ceremonial
quality is still present whenever I go back to Copper Run,
and never more than on that first April trip after a long winter away. Again, I slip and slide my way from the bridge
through those deceptively small riffles; again, I bow through
the hoop of briars; again, the arch of pine forms overhead,
and then, after a quick clumsy cast, my fly line is uncoiling
down across the coppery water in floating N's and straight-
ening in a tug — *two* tugs, the first as the Muddler swings
tight in the current, the second as a trout takes hold with
what can only be described as a hearty handshake of welcome. And just as the arch seems to beckon me each time,
so too when I've passed under the branches it seems to seal
me in. Back beyond the arch is noise and worry and confusion and doubt, but this side of it — stream side of it —
there is nothing but that shiny, exuberant mix of rapid, riffle, and pool, and no requirement upon me but to align
myself with its inspiration and let the current lead me down.

So into the water then — away from the snow and slush
and bad footing and directly into it, frigid as it is. The banks
along this first section are too steep and heavily forested to
balance along, and there's no alternative except to wade. I'm
dressed for it, of course. Woolen underwear, wool pants, silk
liners, heavy socks. For shoes, I wear old sueded boots from
my rock-climbing days, with hard toes and heels that absorb
all the bruises and enough insulation to hold the coldness at
bay . . . at least in theory. In actuality, with the water in
the forties, my toes lose their feeling about every fourth
cast, and I have to climb my way out of the stream and

stamp up and down on the nearest boulder for a good five minutes before the feeling is restored.

By the time I've fished through the first pool, if I'm lucky, I've caught my first six trout, perhaps even the same friendly sentinels that were there the evening I discovered it. By about the fourth one I begin to relax. Behind all the anticipation and excitement that lure me here each spring is a darker emotion: the nagging worry that something terrible will have happened and all of it will be gone. Copper Run, the dancing water, the iridescent trout — all gone. It always takes an hour of being immersed in it — of feeling those twin chills merge, the coldness of the water and the happy shivers transmitted by the trout — before my doubts finally vanish and I let myself wholeheartedly believe.

Below the entrance pool the banks taper together and the water drops between rocks in three distinct runs. They come together again at the bottom, then fan out across a broad shelf of granite into a second, slower pool. The water is darker-looking here, deeper, with large mossy boulders that absorb the sunlight rather than reflect it. A good place for trout, only there aren't any. I fish it each time to make sure, but never once have had even the suggestion of a nibble. Is it too exposed to otter and heron for a trout to be comfortable? Is there some hidden interplay of current that disturbs their equanimity? Or is it just that Copper Run trout are too cranky and original to place themselves in a place so obviously suited to their well-being? If nothing else it gives me something to think about, and lets me know the easy successes of the first pool won't be duplicated on the same lavish scale.

As pretty as it is, the first hundred yards of Copper Run are pretty much a warm-up for what comes next. The water

spills from the fishless pool in one of those terracelike steps
that are so characteristic . . . churns itself over a few times
for good luck . . . then deepens to form a bowl that is so
perfectly round and so tropically shaded it's impossible to
look at it without thinking of Gauguin.

If Copper Run is essence of mountains, essence of woods,
then this pool is essence of Copper Run. I've spent entire
afternoons here trying to separate out all the strands that go
into making it so perfect. The smell is one of them; besides
the wet leaves, the thawing earth, there's a sharper, more
acrid smell that is metallic and not at all unpleasant. The
trace elements, I decided — gold and silver tinges scoured
by water from rock.

A short way beyond the tropical pool a small tributary
seeps in. I say *seep* quite deliberately — it's a damp, spongy
wetness more than a definite flow, and it doesn't appear on
any map. Copper Run itself *is* on the map, but only as a thin
scrawl between contour lines, with only the most approxi-
mate relation to its actual course. It's too small to register
properly; its improvisational, quicksilver meanderings are if
anything anti-map. Were I the cartographer in charge of the
New England hills I would acknowledge its chanciness, slap
a Gothic *Terra Incognita* over the entire height of land, and
let the curious and energetic go about discovering it on their
own.

Which, in my stumbly fashion, was exactly what I was
trying to do. The truth is that despite the visits of five years,
I still had only the haziest notion of Copper Run's course. I
knew where the water started: the combination of ponds
there behind me on the ridge. I knew where, via a larger
river, the water ended: an old mill town beside the Connecticut twenty miles farther south. But the things that hap-

pened in between — the twists of its channel, the dark woods it traversed, the possible waterfalls, its junction with larger streams — were for a long time as unknown to me as the headwaters of the Orinoco.

This was not due to any lack of curiosity on my part — quite the opposite. The water I came to seemed so rich in possibility that each yard deserved an afternoon of admiration to itself. My trips were of pilgrimage, not reconnaissance; each pool had to be sat beside, admired, and fished. What with revisiting the familiar pools and lingering over the new ones, about three new pools per visit was the fastest pace I could manage and still get home before dark. Add the fact that between bugs and low water I only visited Copper Run in spring and autumn — add a dozen tributaries that in their miniaturization and mystery were just as alluring — and you can see I had set myself a question mark the erasure of which was beginning to seem a lifetime's work.

That was my resolution for last year: to increase the tempo of my exploration, to force my pace downriver, to learn before spring ended where Copper Run came out. There would be less time spent exploring each pool, less time to fish, but a labyrinth has its own charms, and I was trying to focus back on it to reach some comprehensive understanding of the whole. I knew the spill where the water surged across a fallen hemlock, grooving the wood until its grain seemed to ripple; I knew the falls where the water washed sideways off a mica-flecked cliff; I knew the spots where the spray kicked high enough off the boulders to wet my face, the best fording places, the pools most likely to hold fish . . . and now it was time to thread these beads together in a necklace to marvel at, fasten, and share.

And if I was proceeding downstream in a pleasant geographical blur, I was proceeding in a pleasant historical blur as well. I knew little about the history of Copper Run, though there was little enough history to know. The stone walls that marked the limit of the early settlers' audacity — the stone walls that climb even Slide Mountain to heights awe-inspiring and tragic — end well below Copper Run. Even the surveyor's tape that dangles everywhere in the woods now, fluorescent and mocking, has only reached the fringes of this notch. Between these two limits — the patient, backbreaking husbandry of the past; the easy, land-grabbing mentality of the present — Copper Run sits like a lost world, removed for a good century and a half from the curse of events. The trees grew, then someone cut them, then they started growing again, and all along Copper Run danced its way south, oblivious to any imperatives but those of gravity.

Our exhaustive town history contains only one story from the height of land — the story of a woman who spent her life in the woods as her father's unpaid assistant in a small logging operation. The older people in town can remember seeing her drive a wagon full of logs past the common to the Connecticut — a straight-backed woman who teetered between proud dignity and shy wildness and never lingered long enough for folks to get to know her. I've seen her grave, the last one in a cemetery where everyone else had been buried seventy years before. It stands alone in one corner beneath some birch; in its simplicity, in its apartness, it could stand for all the solitary lives that have escaped history's record.

She died in 1957 — more than thirty years now. In the decades since probably the only big thing to hit Copper Run have been the Vibram soles of my size-twelve boots, stirring apart the moss on rocks that are as old and untroubled as any on earth. Seen in those terms, I was an invasion — a whole new chapter in what so far had been, as far as man was concerned, a relatively blank book. This placed upon me a certain responsibility; it was up to me, in my short visits there, to conduct myself in a manner befitting an explorer — not an explorer hot for commerce, but an explorer out to record what he had found as faithfully as he could, the better to understand the hidden, threatened beauty of this one fragile place.

So what did I find there? What justified those afternoons along its banks that could have been more usefully spent writing short stories or splashing paint across the barn? What was the payoff for those icy immersions? All pretty stuff, but what — a skeptical Queen Isabella might ask — does this newfound land contain?

Pygmies. Bush pygmies eking out a precarious existence high in a forest remote from man. Copper Run trout, to complete my metaphor, are small, not stunted; independent, not docile; shy, but not so shy a properly placed bauble won't lure them from their haunts. Like mountain tribes, they are splendidly suited to their habitat, and have the happy knack of taking on its qualities — not only its coloration but its very element, so that catching a Copper Run brookie is like catching and holding a condensed length of spray.

And since it is pygmies we're talking about here, it's best to dispose of the size question right at the start. An average Copper Run brook trout is six inches in length; a good one, eight inches; a monster, nine. By the time you've adjusted to the miniature pools and miniature riffles, say fifty yards in, the scale has begun to right itself and you understand what a genius Einstein was when he spoke of relativity. In an eddy twelve inches deep, a six-inch trout takes up a not inconsiderable space; in a shadowy forest, its copper richness is not an inconsiderable source of light.

There's another thing to keep in mind: small is not necessarily easy. The trout come willingly enough to a fly, but they're quick, quicker than the current, and it takes near-perfect timing to connect. Then too, for all their innocence, these fish are not gullible rubes; a trout that strikes and misses will not come again. Add to this the sheer difficulty of placing a fly on the water — the protective overlay of blowdown and branches, briars and boulders — and you have fishing that is as challenging in its small way as any other.

For the fly-fisherman, this goes right to the heart of the problem: the chore of keeping your backcast free of the trees. After an hour and perhaps fifty collisions, it hardly seems like casting at all, but a particularly vexatious form of air traffic control; you spend more time looking back over your shoulder than you do looking in front, and any cast that manages to uncoil without hitting branches seems a pretty successful flight. Take a day of this, and you will be left with the illusion you haven't fished the water at all but the air, and your dreams that night are apt to be laced with hemlock-dwelling trout that mock you with their inaccessibility.

I've learned the hard way not to fight this, but to incorporate the obstacles as part of the challenge. Rather than bring a hundred flies along and moan each time one is broken off, I now bring only two — a Muddler and a backup, thereby assigning a definite limit to just how clumsy I can afford to be. I usually manage to snap off the first one by the third or fourth pool, but you'd be surprised at how long that last one stays on. I've climbed my share of Copper Run trees, plunged my hand deep into pools to work feather out of bark, and even occasionally twisted a hook from my earlobes, but never once have I headed home early for the lack of a fly.

The two-fly limit has another happy effect: it simplifies the process, and simplicity is what this kind of fishing is all about. All fishing, both sport and commercial, has about it something of a complicated hide-and-seek, but small-stream brook trout fishing — the fishing that fascinates me — retains the hide-and-seek quality in its most basic, childlike form. Mountain trout spend their lives hiding in an environment that is perfect for their concealment, and what I find so compelling and interesting in fishing for them is the trick of waving a fly across the water and thereby finding out exactly where they are. The fight, the actual landing — for fish this size, none of that counts. It's the first flash I'm after — the brief but exquisite pleasure that comes when a swirl of water swirls suddenly faster and a life from out of nowhere firmly tugs you, shouting "Here!"

In some pools the trout are just where they're supposed to be — the satisfaction is the smug one of knowing their hiding places so thoroughly. In other pools the hiding places are there, but not the trout — my smugness stands chastened. It's beyond these, in the unexplored water downstream, where the game becomes most interesting. That plinth-shaped rock in the current's fringe — there should be a trout right in front or right behind. Is there? A careful

cast, the fly landing perfectly, the current sweeping it
down . . . No. That log aslant the bank with the deep pocket
along its head. There? Yes! and a good one, all splashing
iridescence, to be brought quickly to my feet, defeathered,
and urged gently home.

Once this simple curiosity is satisfied, there's room left
for a whole complicated superstructure of conjecture and
wonder. Why do Copper Run trout seem to migrate with
the seasons and in a direction reverse to what you might
anticipate, heading upstream when the water turns colder,
downstream when it warms? What autumnal hint triggers
their color change, when their copper deepens toward crim-
son and their spots take on a vivacity that makes even maple
leaves seem dull? Why does their size seem to diminish the
farther from the road you go? Why will they smash a dry
fly and not rise, at least perceptibly, to a living insect? Why
this, why that, and then suddenly I've raced through three
new pools and some pretty connecting water, and my wondering has run away from me and I find a dry, sunny spot
to climb out of the water and rest.

There are several of these resting places along the
stream — flat, grassy terraces just big enough to admit my
outstretched body, slanted so I can stare at the water while
flat on my back. Removed from the iciness, plied with
oranges, I am free to devote myself, for a few minutes anyway, to one of those vast metaphysical questions that only
occasionally seem worth the asking. Why, if I am so
enchanted with the sheer beauty of this stream, must I bring
along a rod and reel in order to fully appreciate it? Why can't
I just stroll down its banks in simple adoration? Why, when
you come right down to it, fish?

There's a teasing, quicksilver-like quality to Copper

Run — like any stream, the moment you try to grasp it, it's gone. And so too with any question posed on its banks; the best you can hope for is a partial, impressionistic answer that leaves in the air as much as it settles. Still, fishing for brook trout on a small mountain stream is about as simple and pure as the endeavor becomes, so that motives stand out with a clarity they lose in bigger, murkier waters.

Why fish? Leaving out on one side the obvious reasons like being outdoors and the healthy exercise, and leaving out on the other side the complicated reasons of blood lust and the ancestral promptings of our watery origins, I think I can begin to find the beginnings of an answer. It has to do with the exploring I mentioned earlier — that ritualistic, challenging version of hide-and-seek. Fly-fishing is the only means I have to enter into the hidden life of a stream and in a remarkably literal way, so that if my cast has been a good one and my reflexes sharp, that life — through the energy of its fishy emissary — pulses up a taut leader through a taut line down a curved rod to my tensed arm . . . to my arm, and by the excitement of that conveyance to my heart. A fishless stream might be every bit as beautiful as Copper Run, but it's the fish that whet my curiosity, stocking it with a life I need to feel to understand.

Discovery, and the vicarious thrill that comes with having my surrogate self — my Muddler, Royal Wulff, or Cahill — go swimming off through a pocket of rapids, being at one and the same time an extension of my nervous system and an independent, unpredictable agent of free will. Like *Alvin*, the tethered submarine guided by cables through the *Titanic's* wreck, the fly answers our commands and does our probing; in some mysterious, sympathetic way we *see* through our fly and understand the water better beneath it than we do the water we're actually standing in twenty yards upstream. That little back eddy near the alders, what's under it? Sweep the rod to the correct angle and our surrogate drifts over and checks it out. That granite reef sunk beneath the brightness? Shake some line loose and our surrogate plunges down.

Our nerves are transmitted to a tethered cell of tinsel and feather — that and the added, exhilarating bonus of knowing any second we may be jumped . . . that our surrogate selves are liable to be eaten. Anyone who compares fishing to hunting has got it backwards; it's the thrill of *being* hunted that gives fishing its charm. For the few seconds our lures swim beneath the surface we recapture the innocence — the dangerous, stimulating innocence — of the days when man walked the earth not as master but as prey. It was, it is, a dangerous thing to be a human, and we need to be reminded from time to time not only of our abstract mortality, but of a mortality that springs from ambush and clamps down.

Why fish? Notes toward the start of an answer, not the answer itself. In this resting place, beside a small ribbon of water on a fine April day, it's the best I can do.

I balance my way onto a rock in the center of the current and begin casting again. With the sun going down, the chill more penetrating, it's time to admit something I've tried to keep from my story as long as possible. The fact, the sad inescapable fact, that Copper Run is threatened, and by the time you read this its miniature perfection will almost certainly be gone.

This will come as no surprise. Here in the last decade of

the Twentieth Century it has become a given that something beautiful is something threatened. A beautiful marriage, a beautiful custom, a beautiful place. We cannot admire any of these without hearing a meter in the background ticking off borrowed time. If that something is remote, fragile, and cherished, then it is doomed even more — there are garbage dumps on Mount Everest, for instance, and the Borneo rain forest is being ground into pulp. Our century has extracted its share of payment over the years, payments social, political, and environmental, but not yet the full amount. The day of reckoning is approaching, and before it, like a glacial moraine, comes the huge debris of extinction, this heavy, pervasive sense of doom.

We're a race of Cassandras now, not Pollyannas, and I have no wish to gloss over the facts. For the corner of New England woods I love the threat is quite simple on one hand, quite complex on the other. The remote notch Copper Run drains is owned by a paper company that is in the business of selling trees. The trees along Copper Run, the trees that entangle my backcasts and darken the riffles, are fast approaching a marketable size. All winter long, as I sit typing, trucks roll past my house loaded with logs. It is too much to expect that none of them will be from Copper Run. The vague uneasiness I experienced last April was not without reason; here spring is approaching again, and yet when I think of returning I feel not anticipation but only dread.

This is not the place for a lengthy discussion of the pros and cons of timber management. Timberland, at least for the time being, is land not being developed or macadamized, and in this part of the country the paper companies have traditionally allowed public access to the woods. Still, any orga-

nization whose sole raison d'être is greed cannot be trusted
to do anything except be true to that principle on any and
all occasions.

As it turns out, I know the man who owns the company
that owns Copper Run, at least by sight. He's in his fifties,
balding, of average height and weight, fond of wearing the
rumpled chinos and flannel blazer of the perpetual Ivy Lea-
guer. He doesn't appear particularly greedy; occasionally,
I'll hear him joking with our postmistress when I go to pick
up our mail. It's hard, looking at him, hearing him laugh,
to connect his appearance with my happiness — to know at
a word from him, at a tuition bill due for his son, some ready
cash needed to float a new deal, a political contribution to be
made, Copper Run and all its treasures could in the course
of a day disappear . . . disappear, and that were I to protest,
the whole weight of law and custom is there behind him to
prevent any appeal.

And yet he looks perfectly harmless; he even drives a car
smaller than mine. At night when I drive past his house all
the lights are on in every room — every room, every light,
no matter how late it is, and I feel a hollow spot in my stomach when I see this and know with a certainty beyond reason
that Copper Run is doomed.

Taking the long view, I can reconcile myself to this, at
least partially; cut forests eventually grow back. But it's
another characteristic of our age that the threats come shot-
gun style, so that even if you dodge one projectile, there are
enough left to cause serious damage. The threat of development, constant road building, the dangers posed by the
warming of the atmosphere and acid rain . . . all these make
cutting seem positively benign. Even my own walks along
the banks must be included in the dangers; as careful as I

am, as gently as I bring them to hand, there are trout that die when you hook them, and the loss of even three or four good fish a season, in an environment so fragile, is the equivalent of a major kill. Like Steinbeck's Lenny, that animal-loving fool, we can hug the things we cherish until they die.

But here's where the complexity enters in. Just as there is a real Copper Run faced with real, mortal dangers, so too there is an abstract Copper Run faced with dangers that are abstract but no less mortal. I refer to the relentless, vicious attack on the beautiful that is going on all around — an onslaught so widespread and successful the only conclusion to draw is that its goal is the destruction of the very notion — the very *humane* notion — of Beauty itself.

Like the environmental dangers mentioned above, you can make your own list. The brutality and trivialization of popular culture; the abominations posing as architecture; the not-so-coincidental fact that the richest society the world has ever known is also its ugliest . . . all you have to do is look out the window. And though on one hand a sterile glass box designed for the entrapment of a thousand office workers in Indianapolis, Indiana, would seem to have very little to do with the fate of an upland stream in the New Hampshire woods — the mindless, flickering images these office workers watch with their children on a glass screen when they go home even less — the connection is a direct one, it being, when it comes to Beauty, one world after all.

For if Beauty dies in the mass, how can it be expected to live in the particular? How can I possibly describe to that caged-in, image-drugged man sitting there in Indianapolis what a hemlock twig looks like spinning its way down a Copper Run riffle — how the reflected sunlight welling up from the bottom enlarges it so the needles drift within their own delicate halo? How can I explain how a Copper Run trout, held against the palm in the moment before its release, will send a shiver through you that for one fleeting second reconciles you to everything? How to explain all my love for this? How?

A person who writes for a living deals in the raw material of words. And, like rivers, mountains, and forests, words themselves are under attack, so that even the means to describe the desecration are fast disappearing. The gobbledygook of advertising, the doublespeak of bureaucracy (*beautification* for something made uglier; *restoration* for something lost), the self-absorbed trendiness that passes for literature; the sheer weight of illiteracy . . . again, the wretched list. Words like *lovely* and *fragrant* and *natural* have been inflated so far out of proportion they form a kind of linguistic freak show where words that were once suggestive of all kinds of richness now mean something grotesque. Emerson's "Every word was once a poem" becomes, in our century, "Every word was once for sale."

Again, the connection to Copper Run may seem a subtle one, but again it is simple and direct. For the devaluation of words makes for a devaluation of the things words describe and sets up a vicious circle from which there is no escape. With fewer words left to describe our Copper Runs, it becomes harder to justify saving them; as the Copper Runs vanish, the need for a language to describe them vanishes as well.

To a writer — to a dealer in raw materials — a polluted, unreliable source is the worst of calamities. But while the assault on words is every bit as depressing as the assault on the environment, at the bottom is to be found a strange kind of exhilaration, at least for those with the spirit to fight back. For perilous, degenerate times put a great responsibility on those who care for what's threatened, and endow their actions with a significance that is not just symbolic.

Here is where the link between these separate conservations becomes clearest — the conservation of Copper Run, the conservation of Beauty, the conservation of words. For just as the world has seen the wisdom of creating refuges that are as far as possible removed from the hand of man, the better to protect the lessons of untrammeled life, so too should writers seek to create a refuge of words where notions of Beauty and joy and solitude will endure in the very heart of a despoiled language, so that even if the worst happens and our methods of expression become as vacant as our method of living, there will still be books and stories and descriptions to go back to so we can see exactly what has been lost — so we can see these things and so there will remain a gene pool from which Beauty might flourish once again.

I spend my life writing fiction; among other things, it presupposes a certain ability of imagination. If I could, I would have no scruple in making Copper Run imaginary, giving it a make-believe course through make-believe woods protected by make-believe laws in a kingdom of my own design. But an imagination that seeks only escape is no imagination at all, and the best I can do . . . the best I can hope for in these twenty-odd pages of celebration and lament . . . is to state the dangers facing Copper Run as simply and directly as language can manage, and thereby protect, if not this wild upland province, at least this wild, upland province of words.

*   *   *

An ending, and yet not the end. For now it is April again, and I have gone back to Copper Run to find it only slightly changed. The trees are a little higher, a little thicker, but still uncut; the trout are smaller, but they seem just as plentiful; the water, while it may be more acidy, still vaults across the boulders in happy leapfrogs, and the sunlight still takes on that grainy, shaftlike quality as you go deeper into the woods. I retrace it pool for familiar pool, moving so slowly there's only time this first trip for a small portion of new water: a bright rapid surging between matching boulders overhung by a giant spruce.

Only one new step, but who knows? Maybe this will be the year I keep my resolution and follow Copper Run to its junction with the larger river to the south. It can't be far, and it's only my enchantment with what I've discovered that keeps me from pushing ahead at a faster rate.

Will I be disappointed to find an ending? I don't think so — well, only partially. For if the Copper Run I love is finite after all and joins a woods road or path I've already traveled, at least I'll have the solace of the pattern's completion. In the end, it's all we can ask of the unknown — that it leads us around at last to the familiar and sets us off on the trek once again.

May 12

Started this morning with four pages to go before the end of a story. Striking distance, so I went for it, holding out the prospect of an afternoon's fishing on the Waits to urge me along. A cool sunny day. Adrenaline weather.

With Celeste at nine months — with a baby due any moment — there are more preparations to be made than merely grabbing my rod and bolting out the door. The Protestant Work Ethic (branded a scarlet PWE on my soul) is sticky enough at the best of times, but add some incipient paternal angst and the guilt slows you down. Is the phone working? The obstetrician's number written down in plain sight? The extra car full of gas? The neighbors at home and alerted?

Celeste, who is managing just fine thank you, finally shoos me out the door. Call you every hour, I tell her . . . which turns out to be a lot harder than it sounds. Always before I had thought of the half-hour drive up to the river as a progression past a familiar, pastoral set of landmarks. The bridge over a Connecticut rolling gently in the sunlight; Gray's auction barn with its holding pens and pensive cows; Morey Mountain with its beetling cliffs; half a dozen farms, each field greener than its predecessor, each barn more eccentric in its windowing and sheds. Now, anxious, I see the drive strictly as a succession of phone booths, or rather a desert of them. I find one by an abandoned railroad station, quickly dial home — situation normal. There's a long stretch without any, so I pop into an antique store and beg the use of theirs — again, nothing at home has changed. A thirty-mile stretch of Vermont with only one pay phone? I'd never thought of the landscape in those terms. A bad country for spies, philanderers, and expectant dads.

One of the things I love about the Waits is how it comes into sight suddenly, the road making one fast left-to-right swerve. Voilà. It's high, but clear, the midstream rocks covered in clean purpled shadowings. Perfect shape for early May. Parking by the pool called the Aquarium, pulling on my waders, I formulate Wetherell's First Law of Fishing: *That the success or failure of a fishing trip is determined by the ease or lack thereof with which a fly line is threaded through the guides of one's rod.* For a change I do it smoothly, without missing a guide or having the line sag maddeningly back through the seven I'd already threaded. Add to that the ease with which I tie my first blood knot of the day and all the auguries are favorable.

As well they might be. I wade out into the middle of the current at the base of a broad pool; the water, catching my legs, finding my waist, gives me the same surge of togetherness that comes with donning a new pair of jeans. All spring I've been trying out a new act on the smaller streams: a weighted nymph fished upstream with an indicator. Now, with the water level high, streamers not producing, I'm ready to open, as it were, on Broadway.

It's a weighted Hare's Ear I'm using, though from the look of it a hare's turd would be a better description. The indicator — a sticky fluorescent press-on of orange — goes around the leader eighteen inches up from the fly. The whole rig is cast clumsily upstream. The orange press-on bobs around a bit, aligns itself with the current, then starts downstream like a guide scouting out the river for the timid nymph. If the orange suddenly stops — if, better still, it suddenly dips below the surface — you strike hard with your rod and thereby hook, in textbook fashion, your nymph-feeding trout.

Which, to my amazement, is exactly what happens. Not only once, but seven times in a row. Cast, orange stop, *fish*. Cast, orange disappear, *fish*. What's odd about the whole process is that, unlike fishing with a dry fly or streamer, there's a built-in delay between the time you strike and the time the fish is felt — a fish that is, after all, swimming *toward* you in order to catch the nymph. Thus, it's hard to know who's more startled: me to find the trout is attached; the trout to find he *is* attached. The fight doesn't take long as a result — the trout all but raise their fins in surrender. I twist the barbless hook out and off they swim, a new lesson stamped upon the miniaturized, solid-state computer chip of their brains.

It's a lot of fun. No, more than fun — exhilarating. To have a new method by which to explore my river, to probe riffles and currents where I've never been able to raise a fish before. Exhilarating! There's something in the enterprise reminiscent of fishing a bobber with worms for sunfish, and takes me back to those eleven-year-old days when all my longing, all my hope, was pinned on that little plastic bubble of red and white — on intensely wishing for the moment it would give a tremulous side-to-side quiver and abruptly sink.

Law Number Two. *We fish for our childhoods.*

I continue to catch fish all afternoon, though never so easily. More than fish. Those old stock cartoons of a fisherman pulling up a dilapidated shoe? I've never caught a shoe, never so much as a sneaker, but on one drift my nymph manages to snag the rubber lid of a mason jar, souvenir of some farm wife's autumn canning. At four it begins to rain, but I keep at it until trees, fields, stone walls, and sky are washed into the same gray intermingling.

It's been five hours since I called home. When I arrive there it's to the aftermath of mass hysteria. Cars parked on our grass, people running about, a man toting a camera. One suggestive touch: a baby carriage on our front porch complete with freshly plumped quilt! I rush inside, ready to apologize for not calling, ready to boil water or coach breathing exercises, my emotions a churn of guilt, anxiety, and pride.

But there is no baby, at least not one that's ours. Celeste is in the parlor talking excitedly with a friend from up the road who cradles their three-month-old on one knee. The scene outside is quickly explained. A moose — a young male — had wandered down through the village, stopping traffic, causing a mad rush for cameras. The moose, head tilted in bemusement, sauntered past the post office, then

crossed the road and began eating the flowers in our neighbor's garden . . . or at least sniffed at them as if he would
like to eat them.

Tulips. The old Unicorn in the Garden syndrome.
Celeste, walking carefully, takes me over to show me the
evidence of the trampled stems.

River of Rivers

It's a fish story that starts on dry land, the stretch of Route 11 that drops from Peru to Manchester like a gigantic slide. A water slide to be exact — it was May and raining hard. I was on my way to the Battenkill for my annual visit, and to pass the drive had slipped into the cassette player one of those rare inventions that helps justify our age: a tape-recorded book. In this case, it was the short stories of John Cheever, and not just any Cheever, but "The Swimmer," in which suburbanite Neddy Merrill decides to swim the eight miles home from a cocktail party via neighborhood swimming pools.

"He seemed to see, with a cartographer's eye, that string of swimming pools, that quasi-subterranean stream that curled across the country. . . . When Lucinda asked him where he was going, he said he was going to swim home."

It's a classic story, read well by the reader, and if nothing

else it made me slow down enough to fit the ending in before
the snarl of Manchester traffic. By the time I was down to
Arlington, the tape was over and the sun was out again, sil-
vering the raindrops that clung to the guardrails and trees.
My mind, so absorbed in Neddy Merrill's problem, only
gradually switched focus to W. D. Wetherell's: Battenkill
browns and what they would be in the mood for after a
week's steady rain.

I parked near the store in West Arlington, and within
minutes was up to my waist in cold water, false-casting an
antique Honey Blonde toward a hemlock that tilted over the
current like a finger pointing "Here!" It was good to be in
the Battenkill again — good to see those deceptively lazy
folds of water come sweeping past, making me think as they
always do of an exquisitely fine silk being ceremoniously
unrolled.

And it was good, or at least not that bad, not to catch
trout right away. The Battenkill being the Battenkill, there
were no suicidal trout waiting around to hurl themselves
onto my hook, so after an hour without a bite, it was
obviously time to forget my literary daydreaming and put
some effort into the enterprise.

I switched to a Muddler, began paying more attention,
and yet a part of me was still off in Neddy-Merrill-land, so
that as the fishless casts began mounting up, I began con-
cocting a Cheeverish fantasy of my own. What flashed
before my waterlogged brain wasn't a chain of swimming
pools (yuppies or no yuppies, there still aren't that many in
Vermont), but a chain of trout streams. Would it be possible,
I wondered, to travel all the way around Vermont, all the
way up the Champlain Valley, across the Green Moun-

tains, down the Connecticut, and never once leave a trout stream? To fish clockwise around the state and never touch dry land?

Two images immediately came to mind, the first super-imposed over the second in a graphic overlay: the vivid sharpness of a Vermont state road map, with its twisty red highways and even twistier blue streams; the vaguer, hazier, but no less real map of memories I've garnered in fishing several dozen Vermont trout streams over the course of the past twenty years. On the matter-of-fact level where they met, it was clear that to fish one stream into the next and never leave water was impossible. You could come close, tantalizingly close, but eventually each river would end on a height of land separating it from the watershed in the adja-cent valley. What *was* possible, though, was to drive around Vermont and never be more than a few miles from prime trout water, setting up the possibility of an around-the-state trip fishing each river in turn. As a stunt, you might be able to do it in two full days, three if you lingered a bit over the scenery. Thirty rivers in three days? It was a nice idea for a future expedition, say in the indeterminate future of post-poned dreams and procrastinated projects I always refer to as next "autumn."

Back to the fishing. While my mind was busy computing mileage and routes, my Muddler was taking a leisurely swim downstream toward some alders overhanging the undercut bank. Forty feet upstream, still daydreaming, I stepped around a saucer-sized pool of sunlight, scaring up a good-sized brookie. I cursed, mad at my clumsiness, and was start-ing to strip in for my next cast when there was a heavy tug on my line in the direction of the vanished Muddler.

I struck immediately back, half expecting to find I'd

hooked a canoe or at least a good-sized inner-tubist. But it was neither of those things. The water, heretofore so silky, splintered upward like a burst piece of metal, and through the hole where the river had been appeared the snout, the Muddler-festooned snout, of the largest trout I'd ever seen, dreamed, or read about — a once-in-a-lifetime trout, that is; a butter-flanked-hooked-jaw-monstrous-old-granddaddy Battenkill brown.

A *smart* Battenkill brown. The moment he felt the hook he set off in the direction of Sushan, stripping off thirty yards of line before the significance of what was happening to me fully sank in. I started off in pursuit, running through the shallows as fast as my waders permitted, every now and then staring down anxiously at the bare spots in my reel where the backing was disappearing fast. It was obvious now that the brown was trying to pull the old cross-the-border trick on me. I had no New York license, and once he made it around the tight bend that uncoils across the state line he would be safe.

Risking everything, I hauled back on the rod. The trout, startled, pranced across the water on its tail like a sailfish. My leader made the ominous pinging sound wire makes before it snaps, but — miraculously — it held. The brown raced upstream past me, giving me just enough of a glimpse to turn my legs to syrup. Fifteen pounds, I remember thinking. Fifteen pounds!

I ran upstream after him, retracing our route, getting into new water above the covered bridge, then making it into that classic tree-lined stretch that parallels 313. There were a lot of fishermen about, and they scurried to the banks to make way for us, calling out encouragement and advice. I felt pride and embarrassment both — the fish, after all, was playing *me*. "Give him line!" one fisherman shouted; I wasn't sure, but he seemed to be shouting this to the trout.

We were already up to the curve where the river approaches Route 7 and heads north. The soles of my wading shoes, thin already, were wearing out fast on the rocks and briars along shore. The trout showed no sign of weakening; if anything, the colder, faster water where the Roaring Branch comes in seemed to invigorate him, and he increased his speed to something phenomenal. Luckily, there was an old Grumman canoe lying abandoned on the shore. In a flash, I was into it, and, instead of chasing the trout along the shallows, let him tow me in comfort up the center of the main stream.

It was a wise move, at least at first. We were into that beautiful, unwadable stretch below Manchester suggestive of a river lazing its way through the château country in the south of France. It would have been sticky going without the canoe, and the extra drag on the trout — the sea-anchor effect — slowed him up by a full knot. Unfortunately, the river as we approached the Equinox Golf Course began to shallow out, forcing me to abandon the canoe again and start after him on foot.

Somewhere to the left was Orvis headquarters, and I had half a mind to tether my trout to a tree somewhere, rush off, and ask my friend Tom Rosenbauer for advice. Tom knows more about trout fishing than any ten men I know, and what's more he knows how to have fun while fishing, an even rarer quality. I was just deciding I'd have to manage without his help, when who did I see cheering me on from the riverbank but Tom himself! He was waving a pen at me, shouting something that sounded like "Make him talk! Make him talk!"

Tom might be able to make trout talk, but not me. I chased mine upstream past the falls in Manchester Center (over which he leapt with salmonlike ease) to the cheers of shoppers in the street above. The trout, shied by the traffic noise, continued straight up the Battenkill through town. There was a moment when I thought he might veer off into the West Branch, try to force his way to the Mettawee back toward New York, but a subtle tug on my part kept him on the main river. I raced after him, tired now but feeling a lot more optimistic than I had since Arlington. It was clear that the trout would soon run out of water to thrash around in — that at the point where the Battenkill becomes a brook hardly deep enough to support a chub, the trout would beach himself on a sandbar and be mine.

Mine? It is to laugh. For it was here, where the Battenkill vanished, that the trout proved what a truly extraordinary creature he was. An ordinary trout would have surrendered at this point, turned belly up and finned toward my net. A brighter than average trout might have tried to make the leap into Emerald Lake, swim across it in a futile attempt to reach the headwaters of Otter Creek. What my trout did — what this fabulously huge, fabulously intelligent trout did — was make a flopping, jackknife motion with its middle, wiggle up onto the bank across some pine needles, then — my Muddler still attached to his lip — start cross-country through the rain-soaked lowlands heading north.

I scarcely trust my memory here, so surprising was this shift in the trout's strategy. I've caught my share of fish over the years, but never one that did its fighting on dry land. Still, there was no use standing there feeling sorry for myself. I loosened the drag on my reel, hitched up my waders, and started after him. Rather than force his way through the raspberry bushes, he elected to follow the railroad tracks that parallel Route 7, flip-flopping from tie to tie. It was tough keeping him in sight, but after a mile of this he changed tactics again and squirmed through the puckerbrush over to north-flowing Otter Creek.

Fine, I decided. Otter Creek gave me roughly one hundred miles of water to play him in, and if worse came to worst I could land him in Lake Champlain. We were up to Danby now; as if reading my thoughts, the trout veered east into the first tributary we came to: the beautiful Big Branch, one of my favorite mountain streams. Besides its impressive gorge, an interesting stretch of Long Trail, its wild rainbow trout, it boasts one of the truly great assemblages of boulders ever deposited in one spot. It was through these that my trout was now porpoising, heading directly east past Mount Tabor into the heart of the Greens.

Fatigue-wise, this was the hardest part of the entire battle. Not only did I have to race upstream, I had to do it over boulders, so that it was more rock climbing than fishing. Somewhere along the way we passed the mouth of the Black Branch, where on a cool October day in 1971 I saw a man with forty-two dead brook trout laid out on a newspaper; the man was smirking proudly, waving hikers over to see, and in his lapel he wore the button of a prominent conservation organization.

I raced past the spot with a shudder, determined now to catch up with the trout once and for all. He went under the suspension bridge below the Long Trail, did a somersault in the next pool, then raced back downstream toward Otter Creek, forcing me to spin around like a clumsy matador, but giving me a good look at his totality. It was gargantuan —

on the scale of the Big Branch boulders. His tail alone was three times bigger than any trout I'd ever hooked!

In some respects, our battles up to this point had been all preliminary; we had been feeling each other out, as it were, and now it was time to get down to some serious fish-playing. Unfortunately, I was currently in a poor spot to exert any pressure: downtown Rutland. Otter Creek being too deep and foul to wade there, I hitched a ride with a passing motorist, sticking my rod out the window and signaling with my free hand which way to turn. By this method, I was able to follow the trout past the State Street Bridge. Some school kids, on their lunch break, began tossing Hydrox cookies down at him, scaring him upstream. We followed, swerving recklessly to avoid oncoming cars. In a few minutes, free of the city, I hopped out, thanked the driver for his help, and began wading through the marshland along the river near Pittsford and the mouth of Furnace Brook.

I was hoping the brown would swerve off into this stream as he had the Big Branch — it's a pretty little river and has a starring role in Harold Blaisdell's fine book *The Philosophical Fisherman*. This trout, however, was not about to grant requests. After the briefest of forays into Furnace, he continued upstream, making similar short runs into the Neshobe in Brandon and the Middlebury ten miles farther north.

The New Haven was the next tributary after that — an excellent dry-fly stream and one I know well. Apparently, the trout thought highly of it, too, for the moment he got to its mouth he sped right up the middle, not stopping until he reached the open stretch behind the Dog Team Tavern. He chased his tail in ecstasy for a good ten minutes here, drunk on the smell of sweet rolls emanating from the restaurant's kitchen. The smell was a nostalgic one for me, too. As a freshman at Middlebury back in the Sixties, I would hitch rides north to fish the New Haven, cutting class to do so, hitching a ride home again after a long, trout-filled afternoon.

There were lots of memories here, both of people and days. My friend Murray Hoyt, a fine writer and a gentle man; Murray, who loved the New Haven as much as I did, and when someone asked him how the fishing was, would take the single good trout he'd caught out from his creel, hold it up for admiration, put it back in, then pull it out again, repeating the performance three or four times. The willow-shaded pool near the cemetery below Bristol Flats where on a hot August afternoon of joy and crushing disappointment, I hooked and lost the biggest trout I'd ever seen prior to the one I fought now. The stretch above the swimming hole where in the years before development it was possible to take a dozen iridescent brook trout in as many casts. The tiny upland cemetery near West Lincoln where, one morning before sunrise during the height of the Vietnam War, I passed a burial in progress, with an honor guard of three uniformed soldiers, a flag-draped coffin, and nothing else — no mourners, no spectators, nothing to disturb the heart-wrenching poignancy of the scene.

It was at this point — racing after the trout where the river climbs the mountains toward Lincoln Gap — that it began to occur to me that the trout was familiar with an unusually large portion of the state. This was startling in its way. You expect a trout his size to have a map imprinted on his brain of every rock, current, and channel in his home river, but to have a map of Vermont imprinted there? It made me curious to see which route he would choose to cross the mountains: the New Haven south toward the headwaters of the White, or the woods overland toward the headwaters of the Mad.

The Mad. In one long plunging sweep he was out of the river, into the underbrush, up and over the old logging roads that crisscross the height of land. At Sugarbush, he took to the ski trail, sliding down on his belly like an exuberant otter to land with a magnificent splash in that big Mad River pool above Waitsfield. My arm at this point felt as if I'd just received six tetanus shots in a row, double strength; my waders, torn from sliding down the mountain after him, flapped indecently. Even so, a new determination had taken hold of me, and by the time we tumbled over the falls below Moretown, I had half convinced myself the trout was beginning to show signs of tiring.

Down the Mad we raced to the Winooski, upstream past the statehouse in Montpelier, up the Dog past those sylvan, gravel-bottomed pools that back the Norwich campus — the trout towing me now, so that I hydroplaned on my stomach back and forth past the startled picnickers, drenching them in spray. I shook the fly line up and down like the reins of a horse, trying to nudge him toward Roxbury and the headwaters of the Third Branch near the hatchery. But no — this trout had an itinerary of its own. Back down the Dog he rushed, up the East Branch of the Winooski through that fine rocky pool by the high school in Plainfield, then into the sandier, high-banked pools below Marshfield farther along. He paused to catch his breath here — I tethered the line to a willow, rushed into the Rainbow Café for some brioche and a Linzer torte — then off we went again heading due north.

Time blurs here. I'd been fighting the trout for the past

five and a half hours, and the strong May sunlight was
beginning to do odd things to my brain. Nevertheless, when
I got home that night I was able to trace our route on a map
with a felt-tip marker, and it makes for an interesting line.
When the trout ran out of Winooski, he went overland to
the chain of ponds near Woodbury, traversed them toward
Hardwick and the Lamoille, followed the Lamoille downstream to the Wildbranch, followed the Wildbranch upstream to the headwaters of the Black at Eligo Pond, sped
north on the Black all the way to Lake Memphramagog in
the heart of the Northeast Kingdom, swam across the lake
to the Clyde, headed up the Clyde south to Island Pond, ran
down the Nulhegan to the Connecticut, up and down Paul
Stream to cool off, up and down the Wells for a bit of sight-
seeing, up and down the Waits for more of the same, back
down the Connecticut to White River Junction, up the
White to the Tweed to Mendon Brook, and so across the
main ridge of the Greens back to Otter Creek heading south.

There's a book's worth of adventures in our two-
hundred-mile odyssey, but of all the memories several
in particular stand out. How the trout danced a cha-cha up
the Clyde near Derby Center. How depressed I became at
the tires and innersprings and bleach bottles tossed down the
stream banks; how that was nothing compared to the dis-
couragement of seeing too many For Sale signs by too many
farms. How lovely the Wells turned out to be, with deep
undercut banks that rolled us out of earshot of the century.
How on the Waits — the lyric, fragile Waits, my home
river — I passed a teenager fishing the pool known as the
Aquarium; how during our brief talk he mentioned a man
had written a book about the Waits and I was able to tell him
it was me. How on the White I spotted my friend Terry

Boone sipping coffee on the bank behind Tozier's; how this conservationist friend of all Vermont trout cupped his hand around his mouth and yelled, "You're going to release that fish, right Wetherell?" How my other fishing friends, Tom Ciardelli, Dick Ayers, Peter DesMeules, and Ray Chapin, stood behind him, nodding their heads in agreement. How below the hatchery in Bethel the salmon parr clustered around my trout as though they had found their long-lost mother. How as the fight continued on into the early evening I began feeling as though I wasn't attached to a fish at all, but a deer or bear — something too mammalian for comfort, so that as we raced down Otter Creek back toward the Battenkill, I began half rooting for him to escape. How I almost had him once on the Tweed — was able to lead him exhausted to the bank, when my clumsy boot poked him in the side and sent him tearing off again.

In Cheever's story, Neddy Merrill swims through so many swimming pools it's all he can do to pull himself from one to the next. "He had done what he wanted, he had swum the county, but he was so stupid with exhaustion that his triumph seemed vague." In a similar manner, I stumbled my way down the Battenkill to the spot where my Muddler had first disappeared back in what now seemed the remote past. Like Merrill, my mind swam in exhausted circles, so I no longer could tell hallucinated trout from actual ones, literal rivers from dream rivers, a Vermont of the imagination from a Vermont that was real.

There ahead of us in the middle of the river now appeared the largest logjam I'd ever seen before — one so huge, complex, and twisted it could only have been built by steroid-drunk beavers . . . and built in the course of a single afternoon. The trout, sensing its chance, made right for the

middle, plunging toward the bottom where the branches
were thickest. At first I was able to hold him — for an instant
the leader ran free — then with a sickening sensation that
was half victory, half defeat, I saw the line stretch, hold,
stretch . . . stretch . . . and snap.

I don't remember much of my immediate feelings; I
think I was too drained to think about much at all. I do
remember looking down at my watch. Ten-thirty, it read.
Ten-thirty A.M. The morning sun had risen enough to erase
the silver from the tree limbs. I shook my head to clear it.
Downstream in the riffle where the logjam had vanished, a
twelve-inch brown rose to a floating mayfly — rose twice,
knocking it down in a splashy second effort. I stripped my
Muddler in and changed quickly to an Adams.

One river at a time, I told myself, working out line. One
beautiful Vermont river at a time.

May 27

Needing some flies, needing a nice zinfandel to go with a picnic we were planning for Memorial Day, needing to have some film developed, needing most of all to spend a few minutes with a man I admire a great deal, I stopped Monday at Lee Chapman's store over in Vermont. I'd call it a general store, if it wasn't for the inspired specificity of the place: rare books marvelously arranged; flies just as marvelously disarranged; bag balm, cough syrup, and other patent medicines; antique gowns and lace doilies collected by his wife, Oddie; the wide selection of wines tended knowledgeably by his son Will. It's a store where you might buy just about anything you want, as long as the wanting stems from something curious, tender, and happy in the human spirit, not something venal, quick, and mean.

Perhaps it's only in retrospect, but something hollow — a vacuum, the actual empty feel of it — was present the moment I swung open the heavy screen door. Oddie and

Will were standing by the counter near the old-fashioned cash register; what they said was said first by their expression.

"Lee died Saturday."

It was the jarring kind of news that can't come as a surprise. Lee had been in and out of the hospital down in Hanover for the past few years; his heart, just because it was so generous, was having trouble keeping up. Saturday night it had finally quit, but not without one last Chapman quip. A few moments before the end, Lee opened his eyes, looked around, saw his family sitting there, and staring right at them said, "My God, am I still here then?"

That was Leland Chapman — druggist, fast squad leader, air force officer, storekeeper, fisherman, hunter, fly-tyer, and friend to an amazing cross section of humanity, from the kids of the village to the movers and shakers of the larger world. I'd written about him in a little book, described him as a "moody Santa Claus" (it wasn't until I knew him better that I realized only the last two words applied), and after the book came out I was a bit apprehensive about how he would take it all. I needn't have been, of course. Lee was tickled pink by his inclusion, and to the shelves of liniment and typewriter ribbons and spinning reels was added several dozen copies of my book.

We talked about fishing a lot the last few years, planned on going out together, but it was one of those things — we never found the time. Now that it was too late I felt guilty and intrusive. After the usual inadequate words — after finding out when the funeral would be — I was starting to leave, when Oddie took me gently by the arm.

"We'd like you to read something at the service," she said.

At first, I demurred. For all the respect I had for Lee, our time together consisted largely of turning through plastic fly boxes, searching for some elusive pattern he wanted me to try. But I was wrong to think this kind of friendship wasn't just as real as one developed over long years. Lee's life was full of such friendships, the friendship that comes in short intense bursts, and as representative of the hundreds of people who knew him this way, I was honored to have a part.

This was on Monday. Today, in brutally hot weather, they held the service in the white Congregational church that stands within casting distance of Lee's store. It was standing room only — the overflow sat out on the lawn. The numbers were matched by the variety. Farmers, leftover hippies, a contingent from the Masons, an honor guard of firemen and police, people in suits, summer folks from the lake, the flamboyantly artistic, the self-effacing and polite. As I stood there waiting to go in, I tried matching each person to the appropriate merchandise in Lee's store, wondering which were the fly-casters, which the book collectors, which the liniment users or connoisseurs of wine.

Lee's coffin was set in the middle of the church, covered with a flag. His family sat in the pews to the right. I slipped into one of the last spaces toward the back, and nervously read through my reading while waiting my turn. The minister did his part, but it wasn't until they came to the portion of the service where his neighbors and friends spoke that the proceedings seemed to have anything to do with Lee. They were funny stories mostly, tender and human. A woman read a poem she'd composed about Lee's love of fishing, and when she finished the minister signaled me and up I went to the pulpit, sweating bullets.

What I read was by Robert Traver, a man whose love of

life mirrors Lee's own. "Testament of a Fisherman," it's
called. Oddie, coming up to me later, said it fit Lee to a T.

I fish because I love to; because I love the environs where
trout are found, which are invariably beautiful, and hate the
environs where trout are not found, which are invariably
ugly; because of all the television commercials, cocktail par-
ties and assorted social posturing I thus escape; because, in
a world where most men seem to spend their lives doing
things they hate, my fishing is at once an endless source of
delight and an act of small rebellion; because trout do not lie
or cheat and cannot be bought or bribed or impressed by
power, but respond only to quietude and humility and endless patience; because I suspect that men are going along this
way for the last time, and I for one don't want to waste the
trip; because mercifully there are no telephones on trout
waters; because only in the woods can I find solitude without
loneliness; because bourbon out of an old tin cup always
tastes better out there; because maybe one day I will catch a
mermaid; and finally, not because I regard fishing as being
so terribly important, but because I suspect that so many of
the other concerns of men are equally unimportant — and
not nearly so much fun.

Last *Voyage* of the Bismarck

Buoyancy is a quality I have always admired, but always from afar. To be carried along on the choppy froth of things, bouncing, floating, skipping, held above the turbulence by an unquenchable welling up — these seem to me in my leadenness the happy pinnacles of joy. Swamped as I am by bothersome detail, weighted down by brooding, ballasted by doubts, it is all I can do to manage a rough treading water, let alone actually float. And though I have never had it tested, I suspect my specific gravity corresponds to that of granite. Solid, Wetherell undoubtedly is. Buoyant, Wetherell definitely is not.

I feel the lack most tangibly when I'm fishing. An awkward enough wader at knee depth, I become positively enshackled when I venture into waters above my waist. The wader fabric clings to me like one of those heavy rubber suits the pearl divers were wont to drown in; my wading shoes

send up vibrations frighteningly similar to those produced
by ball against chain. What makes it worse is my aspiration.
Not content with the shallow, easily wadable stretches, I'm
always reaching out for more — reaching so far that my
right hand furiously false-casts a rod held aloft like a sinking
Excalibur, while my feet — touching nothing — pedal back
and forth like an inebriated duck's.

The ultimate futility of this struck me quite forcibly one
morning several years ago when I was on Franklin Pond. As
usual, I was up to my shoulders in ice-cold water, casting to
brook trout that, as usual, rose a teasing yard from my best
efforts. I went through double-hauls and triple-hauls and
hauls for which no name exists, but they had no effect whatsoever except to chase the trout out even farther; I could
cast forever and not catch a fish. And though the long-term
solution was obvious, it penetrated my waterlogged brain
very slowly, as if having to course the same slow evolution-
ary furrows up which it dawned on prehistoric man.

A boat. Of course. Something to float me out to where
the fish were feeding. Eureka!

For a moment, I let the thought of it carry me away. As
always, the effervescence of that first inspiration quickly
sank into something heavier and dull: the writerly poverty
in which I dwelled. For if I was going to acquire a boat, it
would have to be a modest one. No flashy runabout with
gleaming outriggers, no cedar skiff with loving overlaps —
these were unquestionably too dear. Nor did the "belly
boat" have any appeal for me, that weird bastardization of
waders, inner tubes, and fins that makes a fisherman resemble a cross between a hanging tenpin and one of the lumpier
pea pods in *Invasion of the Body Snatchers*. No, what I

needed was an actual craft of some kind, maneuverable, portable, lightweight, and cheap.

It was in the flash of that first dawning notion that the solution lay. For if I was aping prehistoric man in the similarity of our ends, so too could I ape him in the actual means. Man did not make his first leap from shore in a Ranger bass boat with dual Merc outboards, nor did he shove off in an Old Town ABS canoe. He made the first timid venturing on a raft made of hippo bladders, a glorified and bubbly balloon.

As it turned out, our local sporting goods store had three of the latest models. Inflatable rafts, two-, three-, and four-man versions, propped next to one another on the wall like siblings of steadily increasing plumpness and height. They weren't made of hippo insides, but plastic — plastic that had all the quality and thickness of a ninety-nine-cent beach ball. So although I'd had visions of myself coming home with the kind of durable Avon favored by Jacques Cousteau and amphibious commandos, it was apparent that I was going to have to settle for something considerably less grand.

I examined the rafts more carefully. For something so simple, there was an amazing proliferation of reading matter stenciled across the sides, with extravagant claims of weight-bearing capabilities contradicted by repeated cautions about life jackets. That the rafts were made in Taiwan didn't bother me: the Chinese were an ancient people, and hadn't they invented the junk? The price was reasonable, too, with the two-man model selling for the same price as a dozen bass bugs.

It was the two-man model I finally chose. With a weight-bearing capacity of four hundred pounds, it could carry

Celeste and me with freeboard to spare. The coziness of the actual *sitting* room bothered me (I estimated its measurements at roughly three by five feet), but I let the box illustration override all my doubts. Pictured were *four* bikini-clad models riding the two-man model in what appeared to be not only comfort but also outright joy. Convinced, I went over to the shelves and pulled a box out from the bottom. The actual purchase, for something that was to become so lifelike and personal, seemed anticlimactic and crass. The see-through wrapping, the smell of newness, the exchange of cash. It smacked of buying a child.

I unswaddled it gently when I got home, worried lest any stray pin or splinters puncture it at birth. Spread across the carpet with the flat whiteness of pita bread, it was slow to inflate. (Indeed, the inability of any of a dozen pumps to inflate it in anything less than half an hour was the Achilles' heel of the whole enterprise; the slow *press press press* of foot against bellows was the monotonous cadence of its life.) Only gradually did it grow into a delightful roundness and buoyancy. And round and buoyant is how the raft looked when inflated, with the swelling billow of a magic carpet yearning to be airborne. The contrast between the loftiness of its ambition and the modesty of its means suggested the name. By the time I called Celeste into the room to marvel at what air had wrought, she was *Bismarck*, and *Bismarck* she remained.

Her maiden voyage came that very evening. There's a remote lake on the height of land behind our home that is so wild and lovely I hesitate to even whisper of its existence. Lightly visited and seldom fished, it harbors a fussy population of largemouth bass, some running to size. An old jeep trail runs up to it, but there are no launching ramps, and it would be a long, brutal portage for a canoe. Various row-boats and runabouts have been carted in over the years; their stoved-in wrecks dot the shallows like huge planters deliberately installed for the propagation of lilies.

It was, in short, the perfect place to let *Bismarck* do her stuff. At nine pounds, she was a delight to backpack, and in no time at all, Celeste and I were standing on a granite shelf that slopes into the lake, alternating steps on the air pump. Celeste *oohed* and *aahed* over the scenery; I *oohed* and *aahed* over *Bismarck's* squat lines.

She looked good in the water. Alert, stable, round. Damn good. Even Celeste thought so.

"Why, she's pretty," she said. She rolled her jeans up to wade out to her, then suddenly hesitated. "Uh, how do we get in?"

As usual, she had gone right to the heart of the matter. For *Bismarck,* lovely as she was, was a maddening, ornery, downright impossible bitch to board. The very buoyancy I admired would make her shy away at the slightest ripple, so that approaching her required all the stealth and caution necessary in mounting an unbroken colt. By holding onto the side and bracing my feet against some rocks I was able to boost Celeste into the stern, followed quickly by our fly rods, picnic supper, and wine. By the time all was settled, there wasn't much room left for me.

Correction: no room at all.

"Good-bye!" Celeste yelled, reaching for the oars.

"No, wait a second," I said. "Can't you just . . . scrunch?"

Scrunch is what we did. Celeste tucked up her legs to make a space, I turned sideways and heaved myself up perpendicular to the inflated thwarts, then by judicious wiggling we managed to wedge me in. My first remark was the obvious one.

"It's a good thing we're married."

With our arms intertwined about fly rods, our legs jutting out around each other's chest, I suppose we must have looked like a pornographic carving on a temple devoted to piscine love. I reached for the oars and promptly stroked them into Celeste's chin; she, experiencing a cramp in her right leg, stretched it toward my throat, tipping off my hat. Our fly lines immediately became entangled; the overturned picnic basket leaked pickle brine down over our knees. *Bismarck*, feeling the breeze now, drifted out from shore.

"You sure this is the two-person model?" Celeste asked.

I thumped the lettering. "Here, read for yourself. Two people. Two intimate, acrobatic, contortionist dwarfs. And there," I said, pausing dramatically, "is our bass."

A school of them was tearing apart the lily pads on the far shore in pursuit of — what? Frogs? Shiners? Or was it just their own compacted joy in their bassness, the tremendous joy and lust for existence I sense whenever I have one on the end of my line? We rowed over to find out.

It was a long row. A very long row. *Bismarck*, filled to the gunwales, was not a happy sailor. Halfway there, I fell back in exhaustion. Celeste took over, and by the time we were actually in casting range, collected sweat had added another few inches to the bilge beneath our bottoms.

But that's the sad part of the story. Not another negative word will I inscribe beside *Bismarck*'s name, for once we got to the lily pads we caught bass aplenty, the largest weighing in at over four pounds. *Bismarck*'s good qualities were evident on every one: the stealth and silence of her approach; her low waterline, with its canny view into the bass's own plane; her stability; the ease with which a hooked fish slithered in over her side. By the time we left that night, *Bismarck* had more than justified her existence, and plastic though she was, I already felt that sentimental affinity that can make a boat the most precious and dearly loved of a man's things.

Though Celeste and I continued to play this funny twosie the rest of the summer, it was as a solo craft that *Bismarck* really came into her own. Alone, I nestled into her bottom as if into a soft and yielding waterbed, casting from a comfortably horizontal position, my neck pillowed by the air chamber in the stern. When I was alone, *Bismarck* became a delight to maneuver, responding so quickly to the oars that I often spun her around and around in mad circles just for fun. She rowed quickly and steadily, and seemed to skip under all but the strongest breezes with enough freeboard to keep me reasonably dry. Her lightness and airiness were constant sources of amazement. There were days when I had fish on that towed us halfway across the lake, so that I felt like Ishmael on a miniaturized Nantucket sleigh ride, my mouth dropping open in delight.

What impressed me even more was *Bismarck*'s sturdiness. I fished her hard that summer and autumn, then again the following spring, often taking her out five or six times a week. One of the smaller air chambers developed a leak, but the other three were enough to float her, and I began deliberately seeking out tougher water, to see what she could do. The wide Connecticut in a northwest chop, *Bismarck* bouncing along like a stubby tugboat; huge Newfound Lake, where powerboats threatened to swamp us with their wakes; remote trout ponds, where briars scratched the plastic but punctured her not. . . . We fished them all. There was even one magic afternoon when I found some white water for her — the mouth of a trout stream that empties into the Connecticut. She did well, of course. I backed down the current stern first, and she went bouncing off the rocks like an exuberant pinball, impervious to harm. Confidence expanding, I took her to salt water and tried her out on a windy bay; I took her to a nearby lake in deep autumn when a capsize might have finished us both. *Bismarck* met every new challenge with aplomb.

And the two of us caught fish. Smallmouth that showered her bottom with spray; trout that scissored back and forth near her bow like escorting dolphins; a pike that threatened to puncture us; big walleyes that towed us farther than any bass. Viewed simply as a fishing tool, *Bismarck* proved herself many times over, and I was surprised never to encounter another fly-fisher so equipped. Occasionally, I would see sunburned, angry teenagers paddling along in similar craft near shore, but I never saw one being seriously fished, and most of the time I had to myself whatever body of water I was exploring.

Our partnership remained intact for three full seasons. I had originally thought of her as little more than a disposable boat, to be used several times then discarded like a tissue. Now, her durability proved, I began making the opposite mistake: thinking of her as something permanent and fixed. If I did picture her end, it was always in some cataclysmic happening that would send us both to the bottom in style: a spectacular collision with a spear-shaped rock; a pike big enough to disembowel us; a foot too heavy on the air pump, blowing her to smithereens. That she might die more slowly and subtly never occurred to me at all.

The truth is, she was dying — dying from neglect. By the time that fourth spring rolled around, I had forsaken her exuberant chanciness for the firmer rhythm of a canoe — a fifteen-foot Old Town with a separate beauty all her own. *Bismarck* sailed less and less; for long months altogether, she remained in the backpack, her plastic folds stiffening from nonuse. Occasionally, I meant to take her out, but my back was always aching too much to carry her, or it was too windy, or . . . But why make a list? Excuses count for nothing, not in love affairs, not in boats. She was the apple of my eye, then one day she wasn't, and it's as simple and sad a story as that.

And yet we were to have one more day together after all. It was in May, a weekday afternoon when I felt weighed down with a leadenness that went beyond mere fatigue — as flat as one of those leftover leaves one finds on the forest floor. That I desperately needed a filling of water, sky, and trout was obvious. I started to pull the canoe out of the barn, then — motivated by a sudden, overpowering instinct — went back into the mudroom and grabbed the backpack instead.

Fifteen minutes later, I was hiking up the trail toward Franklin Pond, a bundled *Bismarck* perched high on my shoulders like an eager baby spotting out the terrain. The morning sun had given way to ominous yellow clouds, and I hiked faster than usual in order to stay warm.

The pond sits tight against the slope of the one legitimate mountain our town has. It's about five acres in extent, stocked occasionally by helicopter, and unfishable without some sort of raft. So miniature is it, so silver and round, that the usual analogy is to a gem, though I tend to see it as a bowl instead — a punch bowl cradling the liquefied granite essence of the surrounding hills. Trees reflect on its surface; a breeze will ripple the tops of the surrounding spruce, then drop to strum the water, so that the two waves are never quite synchronized, and the dual shimmers shimmer continuously. So pure is the water, so generous the reflection, that casting into its depths gives the sensation of casting into midair.

I unrolled *Bismarck* on the rough tent platform that is the only man-made structure on its shores. Again, I went through the old familiar ritual of making her waterborne. The slow accordion press of the air pump; the furious shutting off of valves; the precarious launching and more precarious boarding; the quick assembly of oars. It was good to return to something I loved and find it unchanged. Unchanged except, that is, in one important respect. As I stroked my way toward the far shore, feeling her generous and yielding tug, I realized with what can only be described as a sinking sensation that *Bismarck*, my neglected *Bismarck*, was sinking.

Slowly sinking. The long winter in the mudroom with its constant freezing and thawing had opened *Bismarck*'s seams. Water seeped in through a dozen thin cracks — my butt was already numb from icy pond water collected in the stern. It was obvious that *Bismarck* was on her way out, and yet . . . well, it wouldn't happen immediately. The two air chambers that formed the hull were already empty, but a quick check showed that the largest chamber, the outer one, was still partially filled. With luck — if I handled her carefully — *Bismarck* had an hour's float left.

Risky, sure, but there was a compelling reason not to return to shore at once: the trout. Between one moment and the next, as if on an invisible maestro's dramatic cue, they had begun rising on all sides. I worked out some line and immediately caught four brookies in a row on a small Gray Wulff. The lower *Bismarck* sank, the easier it was to slide them over the side, until finally it was hard to determine where pond ended and boat began, and the trout bubbled around my stomach in perfect contentment as I twisted free the fly.

I don't remember how many trout I finally caught. The flies were hatching so fast on the water that the pond literally boiled. A hungry swallow flew down from the mountain, then another, then a third, until finally the air seemed just as thick with darting birds as it did with lazy insects. There were swallows everywhere, coming in squadrons, peeling off, strafing the surface, jetting away. It was a miracle I didn't snag one on my backcasts, but they seemed to be deliberately toying with the line, ducking under it like girls jumping rope. They were teasing me — inebriated with the same airy exuberance as the rising trout and the hatching flies.

Then it began to snow.

Huge snowflakes, falling faster than their size should warrant, tumbling down over the swallows and the flies and the trout until everything became jumbled together in a world where there were no separate planes or spheres of perspectives, but everything was one. Was I casting for flies or for trout or for swallows? Was I fishing water, snow, or sky? Man, trout, bug, or bird? It was dizzying, but I was sinking in it, and I began rowing *Bismarck* toward shore, not from self-preservation, but simply because I needed the ballast of the oars to keep my soul from flying away. As I neared shore, a brown shape glided beneath *Bismarck*'s hull in a rush of fluid and backward-flowing fur: a beaver, and it was too much for me, and I realized for the first time what those nineteenth-century writers meant when they wrote the word *swoon*.

I didn't, of course. I didn't turn into a swallow, and I didn't swoon, and, more importantly, I didn't sink. *Bismarck* and I reached shore together, though by now all that was left of her was a thin plastic pressure against my bottom, her last cradling gasp. She boosted me onto a flat rock within stepping distance of land, then made a final expiring sigh and sank away in bubbles. By the time I pulled her up on shore, her seams were open from bow to stern.

I folded her up more carefully than I ever had when she was whole, then started back down the trail to my car, zig-zagging through snowflakes that spread apart into sun. My thoughts were inflated by the miracles I had just witnessed: I walked so fast and with such light-footed sureness that it was almost as if I had inherited *Bismarck*'s very air. I was . . . yes, there was no mistaking it now. I was buoyant. Buoyant at last.

Bismarck. June 14, 1982–May 5, 1986.

She was a lot more than a toy.

June 18

New Hampshire's an embarrassing state to live in, God knows, what with the reactionary politics; the *Manchester Union Leader* and its gutter journalism; the "Live Free or Die" threat on the license plates (referring less to freedom than to the state's legendary cheapness); the reliance on liquor sales for much of the state's income; the depressing roll call of New Hampshire nonentities who have made it big in Washington, from Franklin Pierce to Sherman Adams to John Sununu; the fact that our most famous native son, Daniel Webster, spent the greater part of his life in Massachusetts; Emerson's jibe about how "the God who made New Hampshire taunted the lofty land with little men" . . . the fact that no one west of Vermont seems to have the slightest notion of where the place is.

There are all these things — and then there is Grafton Pond. It's typically New Hampshire in the best sense of the phrase. Granite shoreline shelving out into astonishingly

clear water; banks shaggy with fir trees; a generous scatter-
ing of islands; the way the whole pond seems to lie not flat
but on an inclined plane tilted toward the bald dome of
Mount Cardigan eleven miles to the north . . . the whole
set in a part of the state that's nestled off the tourist routes,
scruffy, uncondominiumized, unspoiled.

I went over there this morning to get a good helping of
its beauty and to check whether the bass were in close to
shore. They weren't, but it hardly matters. Just to be out
there on the sunny surface, my canoe fitting the water so
perfectly it was as if we were propelled by the impression of
her shadow, was reward enough for the long drive.

Even the blackflies seem to respect Grafton's beauty.
They are there on shore when I arrive, all hot and bothered
and happy to see me, but once I paddle out from the shady
launch area they peel off me like gloom's bitter cloud. I dab
on a layer of sunscreen over the Cutter's, pop one of
Celeste's homemade brownies in my mouth, toss out some
line, anchor my fly rod in the stern, then start west along
the shoreline, threading my way through the shallows that
separate the first big islands.

The Laurentian Shield must look like this, rocky, spruced,
and scrubbed. Even the weeds; they don't lay flat and heavy
but toss in the current like fields of wheat. Up on shore are
old stone walls built by the farmers who lived here a century
and a half ago; where they meet the water they keep right
on going, and with the transparency being what it is, I can
trace them a good fifty yards out from shore, the rocks
growing smaller and less golden the deeper they plunge.
Grafton Pond, for all its naturalness, is man-made, im-
pounded to provide water for a distant town. What I'm drifting over are the remains of a vanished New England, the

rural, self-sufficient life that pretty much disappeared seventy years ago with the paving of the first roads.

As I make the circuit of the pond, hopping from island to island to take advantage of their lee, it's hard not to think of those farmers and their backbreaking toil. Could any of them have guessed, at work on a hot day, loading the stone boat with heavy boulders, whipping up the ox, that the wall they so patiently constructed would one day be the shelter for bass? Would anyone believe it now? That the condos and marinas we cram so obscenely around our lakes will one day be the haunt of minnows, admiring their reflections in the cracked and algae-stained glass? I take reassurance from both notions. To go with all its beauty, Grafton has a bittersweet, haunted air; floating over these walls is like floating over a poem by Robert Frost.

There are lots of smallmouth in the pond, either out amid the rocks of the islands or in among the fallen trees toward shore. I've caught three-pounders here in the past, thick and sassy, but today the big ones seem to be sulking. The high barometer probably — so exhilarating to me, it depresses bass no end. All I manage is an occasional bluegill . . . not that there is anything wrong with that. Sunny, fat, and fierce, the bluegill is a noble fish, and I wouldn't mind having been one in a previous incarnation.

It's funny about the fishing. A year ago I would have tried every bug and streamer in my box, tormented every last inch of shoreline with casts, and — not catching much — let the poor results pretty much ruin my day. Today, though, catching fish seems almost beside the point, and I'm content to try a lazy cast now and then and put most of my effort into watching.

This is the year I'm devoting to puzzling out the fishing

motive, so it's worth trying to decide what causes this new
serenity. Is it the birth of our daughter? The fact that having
now spawned (to stay in metaphor) I find my predatory urge
much duller than before? Is that what all these hours spent
chasing fish are about, a sublimated, ersatz sort of fathering?
Does the fishing urge, like so much else, come down in the
end to the sexual one?

Murky depths, too murky for a pond so clear. I paddle
faster, drowning out the philosophical in some good honest
sweat. While most of Grafton's islands lie clustered in a convoy near shore, there's one that sits alone by itself out in
the middle, as if demonstrating to the others what real
islandhood is all about. There in a cove on its near side is a
splashing commotion, and I head over to see what's what.

It's a family of otters — five I can count. My canoe
doesn't seem to bother them, though it's clear they're aware
of it; they turn a synchronized somersault, then shift their
shenanigans a few rods farther out into the pond. Seeing
them at play is like watching an allegory by Edward Hicks,
and gives me another boost of optimism. The otter shall
frolic with the fisherman, the lion lie down with the lamb —
on Grafton Pond anyway, on this one perfect June day.

Watching this, feeling the sun on my face, the spray kick
off the bow and wet me, I realize something else that father-
hood has given me: the gift to see all this as *new*. My daughter is a month old — it will be years before we can bring her
safely out in a canoe — and yet for me her perception is
already the measure of the pond's beauty, and just in time,
too, because my own abilities when it comes to perception
are fast beginning to wane. As a boy and even into my thir-
ties, I could stare enchanted at a perfect cloud or sunny
waterscape for long minutes and be content. Now, thickened

with life's trivialities, distracted by disappointment, hurried, my own senses perceptibly dulled, I find it harder to take such sheer undiluted pleasure in "mere" scenery. But here is the possibility of escaping all that and starting fresh. Not just in the fictional empathies that are such a large part of my life, but every day, in the most commonplace ways, by this vicarious, fatherly looking-out . . . to see as Erin sees.

I have them waiting at home, my wife, my daughter. Around five, after a long day's drifting, I begin to wonder what they're doing — how to put my gentle adventures into words and bring them back to my family intact.

Big (Smoky) Sky

As fiascos go, this was the worst — worse even than the time I landed in Ireland during the biggest snowstorm in forty years and sat eleven hours on a stranded train between an alcoholic priest from Boston, a homesick construction worker from Ohio, and a garrulous professor of Italian at Trinity College, Dublin; worse even than the time I went out to British Columbia for two weeks of mountain climbing and broke my arms falling over a six-inch-high fence my first day there. Worse because warned by both disasters I should have taken out an insurance policy against disappointment and thereby been armed.

In a sense, I had. I knew about the forest fires. All summer the papers in the East had been full of them, each new article revising upward the amount of Yellowstone acreage involved. On Labor Day, two days before I was due to leave, I spent the afternoon on the phone to Montana, calling park rangers and tackle-shop owners and game wardens trying to find out exactly how bad the problem was. All my contacts were very patient with me, took pains in describing the current situation, and were quick to suggest others I could call to learn about conditions in adjoining watersheds. Most of them agreed that (1) the fires were bad, particularly in Yellowstone; (2) the rivers were critically low from the summer's drought; (3) despite 1 and 2, the fishing, at least on headwater streams, was the best it had been in ten years.

Before most trips I find myself looking for excuses not to go. The inertia of a settled life, my history of disaster, the disturbing, impossible-to-erase remnants of the chronic homesickness I suffered as a child — these are all excuses for not putting any part of myself at risk. But this was no ordinary trip — it was to Montana, mecca of American fly-fishing even when all the advertising promoting it as such is discounted, a land so vast filled with waters so brilliant it would expand my notion of riverine beauty in one overwhelming flash. And it was no ordinary time, either; I would be forty in a month, and it seemed right to treat myself to one last thirty-something adventure that would launch me exuberantly into middle age.

I had my plan all worked out. Starting at Bozeman, I would make a slow clockwise loop around the compass; fish the Gallatin upstream along Yellowstone Park's western boundary, spend a day or two on the upper Madison below Quake Lake, then head over to Dillon to fish Poindexter's Slough and the Beaverhead. The nice thing about this itinerary was that it kept me well in reach of Yellowstone; if the fires let up, if it started raining, I could make a fast raid into the park and try some of the famous water there (even the Firehole, which, given the circumstances, might have been an experience too literal to enjoy). If worse came to worst and the fires were still burning, I could make reservations on the spring creeks near Livingston and thus complete my circuit in style.

It was a good plan, at least in theory, and I full believed in it until I landed in Denver on the late afternoon of September 6. Flying cross-country, the atmosphere had been unusually clear, and I'd gotten a good view of the mustard-colored scars left across the prairies by the summer's brutal drought. It gave the impression — in its extent; in the lifeless way nothing stirred — of a land waiting for a match to be applied to its crusted, hemplike edge.

And then in Denver . . . in my frantic change of planes there; in the quick gulp of air I managed as I raced between terminals . . . the match was struck. Denver's air is always smoggy, but this was something far different that had settled in — an actual pall with an acrid bite. The moment the Bozeman flight was airborne we were immersed in thick, rolling clouds that were far darker and grainier than any I'd ever seen. My seatmate pointed toward them and shrugged; that it was smoke from the Yellowstone fires was too obvious to mention.

The landing in Bozeman was scary enough, God knows, what with the nonexistent visibility and the sensation of descending through a force far too mysterious and powerful for a 707 to handle. The air over the terminal was thick with smoke, and this time, in the carbon reek of it, I caught the cinnamon underline of burning vegetation. It was odd in its effect. All the adrenaline that was building up in me, all the nervous irritation that comes after a long day's flying, and yet after a few minutes on the ground I felt relaxed and strangely soothed.

What my heartbeat was responding to was the smell —

the smell that took me back thirty years to the vanished autumn ritual of burning leaves in the suburban town where I grew up. The memory was ludicrously out of proportion to its source — a burning Yellowstone Park — and yet something of this narcotic, lulling nostalgia lingered on all week, to see me through my perils with, if not equanimity, at least a certain amount of perspective.

But all that was ahead of me. On the shuttle to pick up my car, the driver, a young man named Dave, was quick to rave about how good the fishing was, quick to offer me suggestions on rivers and flies.

"What about the fires?" I said, as we peered up at a stoplight, trying unsuccessfully to make out its color. "As bad as it looks?"

"Nah," he said. "Water doesn't burn."

He glanced up in the mirror to catch my reaction — it was obviously a joke he'd had a lot of fun with.

Then, as he was helping me unload my bags: "September fishing is the best of the year. Tie on a hopper, work the edges, stay out of Yellowstone, and you'll do fine."

I'd been in Montana twenty minutes and already learned one thing: people were either fatalistic about the fires or angry, and it paid to find out early in the conversation which type you were dealing with and gauge your remarks accordingly.

"So you don't think the government's to blame then for letting the fires burn?" I asked.

He shrugged like he had that first time. "Wood burns, Mr. Wetherell. Water doesn't."

Dave's terse optimism was just what I needed. When I went to bed that night at my Bozeman motel, I felt more confident than I had all day. True, the TV news was filled with scenes of a burning Yellowstone, complete with villages being evacuated, overcome fire fighters being borne off on stretchers, and the realistic sound of crackling flames (I could picture a producer back in New York shouting over a bad telephone connection: "Give me more crackle, Smithers! More crackle damn it!"). But still, I was convinced the fires would merely form a vivid backdrop to my fishing, add a little punch to the battle stories I was sure to bring home.

Still on eastern time, excited at the prospect of beginning my trip in earnest, I woke up before five. Packing quickly, I ferried my luggage down to the car. With the smoke, the darkness was total — even the mercury highway lights, those harsh ugly deterrents to night, barely dented the blackness. Conditions had obviously worsened overnight. The smoke had a smothering, heavy quality that made it difficult to breathe. Even worse, the wind was out of the south, hot and desiccating . . . bad news to those thousands of fire fighters who must even now have been heading back toward the fire lines for another day of futile effort.

"Water doesn't burn," I said, remembering Dave's upbeat assurance. I said it out loud and I said it twice.

I headed across the parking lot to the lobby to check out. As I did so, I passed a newspaper vending machine set against the motel's window. Automatically, as I have a thousand times in a dozen different cities, I reached into my pocket for a quarter, dropped it in the slot, reached down, blindly grabbed, tucked the paper under my arm, then went into the lobby to the desk.

There was no sign of the desk clerk. While I waited, I unfolded the paper to scan the headlines.

GOVERNOR BANS OUTDOOR RECREATION IN MONTANA.

Six words, fourteen syllables, thirty-eight letters, and together they spelled one of the worst five moments of my life. I read quickly on, praying there was some mistake, but fate had it spelled out for me right from that wretched opening line.

The governor of Montana, in response to the fires sweeping across the state, has closed all land, public and private, to any unnecessary usage, including camping, hiking, hunting and fishing.

It would be impossible to describe my emotions upon reading this in anything less than four paragraphs. One to describe the sheer disbelief, the way I read and read again trying to end that sentence just one word earlier; another to describe the overpowering, physical sense of disappointment, the way it came over me like a giant's hand shoving me to my knees; a third to describe the vexation and anger, the quick computation of how much money I had poured into this trip, the real sacrifice my family had made to enable me to come; a final paragraph — once the others were written, shed, and done with — to describe the absurdity of it all, the melodramatic, overwritten irony of a man landing in the West to celebrate his fortieth birthday with a fishing trip on the first day in history — the first day ever! — that a Montana trout season was ever prematurely closed.

Only one paragraph — the irony, even after a year, is simply too great to be borne. After what seemed like hours, I put the newspaper back down on the desk. I spoke to the clerk in normal enough tones, paid my bill in cash, then walked back to my car, without the slightest idea what to do next.

But that's the good thing about turning forty — you

have certain defenses. When you're up against the big things in life, be it fire, foolishness, or fate, the best thing to do is fight back with a heavy dose of the commonplace. Among all the surging emotions that had hold of me, I found a homelier one and latched onto it in gratitude: I was hungry, hungrier than I remembered having been in a long time, in urgent need of a decent breakfast.

I drove down the strip into town. The only place open that early was a pool hall/bar that probably never closed. It had that familiar college-town smell of urine and old beer, but at least the counter looked clean and there was a fresh pot of coffee perched on the end.

I ordered an omelet with pancakes on the side. The waitress, bored, went off with my order; the only other person in the place was an old man slouched alone on a stool like a model for Edward Hopper. The *Today* show was on the television above the grill; there were vivid pictures of the flames approaching Old Faithful, and more of that loud, morbid crackling.

Absurdity took full command now. With no one else to talk to, all but bursting with the need for sympathy and advice, I explained my predicament to the indifferent waitress and lifeless old man.

". . . all the way from New Hampshire," I said, concluding. "And now the fishing season is closed? How long is this going to last? Does that mean everywhere or just on state land?"

Both of them listened patiently enough, but all they could do for me was scratch their heads — the waitress metaphorically with a slow, sleepy frown; the old man literally, as if he had never come up against the like. Speechless, we

turned toward the TV set and the glaring orange flames;
surely someone would make an announcement and everything would be fixed.

After a third cup of coffee, I took my troubles out to the
street. There were several possible courses of action, none of
them good. I could fly back East on the next available plane;
prudent from a financial point of view, but to cut and run
before the situation fully sank in would increase the hallu-
cinatory effect even past the point where it was now ("You
went to Montana for a day? Just a day?"). I could head down
to Idaho and try the fishing there; a possibility, though I had
already changed plans so often before coming that I didn't
have much heart for a third effort. I could hang around a
few days and see what happened; a policy of default, but not
a bad policy all the same.

The weather forecast was for rain moving in for the
weekend — this was Tuesday. Five days until rain, a day or
two before the bureaucratic treadmill reversed itself, and
that would bring me up to eight days at the earliest before
the fishing season reopened — and even that was only a
possibility.

What to do?

One of the things I had brought west with me was a list
of contacts and friends of friends to look up in the course of
my trip. One of these ran a tackle store in Bozeman.
Obviously, he was just the man to seek out for advice.

I pulled into the driveway just as he was unlocking the
shop. To say it was a bad time to introduce myself is putting
it mildly; if I was surprised and disappointed by the ban on
fishing, the store owner — whose livelihood depended on
the guiding he did in the fall — was shocked and irate.

"That goddamned gutless governor!" he screamed. "The frigging gutless son of a bitch!"

He would get his lawyer after him, that's what he would do. He would get all the guides and outfitters together and force the state to rescind the ban. The governor was just covering his ass, same as always. He had already closed the bow-hunting season because of the fires, and the hunters had let out such a cry that he was extending the ban to fishermen just so no one could say he was playing favorites. If he was serious about the fire danger, why not extend the ban to loggers and miners? They were still allowed in the woods, and they posed a hell of a lot more fire hazard than a fly-fisherman sitting in a drift boat or wading chest deep in a stream.

His anger — his perfectly justified anger — was awesome in its way; as the flames were to later, it dwarfed my own puny disappointment. Eventually, he mastered it long enough to give me some advice: go ahead and fish, at least for today. The rangers wouldn't be issuing summonses for a while, but just ordering everyone off the water. He sold me a one-day license, then sent me off toward Quake Lake the long way around via Ennis (thereby avoiding Route 191 along the Gallatin, where the fires were said to be bad). When I went out the door he was already screaming at someone in Helena over the phone.

As for me? At least I had a direction now, and an ersatz kind of hope that would do in lieu of the real thing. A few miles out from Bozeman the rangeland begins, and though the smoke kept it hidden behind a gray, gauzy veil, it still resembled the Montana landscape of my boyhood picturing.

The Madison comes into view quickly at the Route 84

bridge, and the sight of it — open, rock-studded, and strong — was sufficiently impressive. There were some fishermen wading the edges by a beached drift boat; clearly, they were either ignoring the prohibition or out too early to have learned it was in effect.

After a quick stop in Ennis (the tackle shops crowded with somber fly-fishermen seeking consolation), I drove to where the Madison leaves Quake Lake. Within minutes I was up to my waist in it, enjoying the cold, clear rush of the current, the interweaving side channels, the generous and willing trout. The Madison, I told myself. The goddamn Madison! In less than a half hour I had caught a dozen rainbows and browns on my old reliable Royal Wulff. In the instantaneous quality of it all, the way the trout seemed queued to welcome me, it was almost exactly the Montana fishing experience of which I had dreamed.

But not quite. There was something missing — there were no mountains in the background, not even hills. The smoke hid the views in every direction but west, and not just any smoke, but smoke with rough, ominous edges that suggested the flames weren't far behind. As I fished, I kept glancing over my shoulder to check where it was, and thereby missed a good many rises. Then, too, fishing illegally is not what it's cracked up to be; rather than providing a furtive, daring pleasure, it's more apt to make you feel sordid — a dirty old fisherman worthy of contempt. Even if it *were* fun, the upper Madison is no river to poach; without streamside trees, a warden can spot you a good mile away.

Which is just what happened. I was starting in on a new side channel, casting to the seam of a pool near a sheltering log, when I saw a jeep pull up behind my car back on the highway. A warden got out — there was no mistaking that hat. He shouted in my direction, but I pretended not to hear and kept on casting, working myself toward a small island and a protective screen of brush. Once past it I waded faster, hoping he would tire of chasing me and go back to his jeep. But this was a forlorn try — a last, pathetic rebellion against the irony that had me squarely in its sights.

"Excuse me, sir?" he shouted, from a short distance downstream.

My first impulse was to raise both hands in the air; my second, to play dumb.

"Oh? . . . Oh, hello there."

I reeled in and waded over to the bank. He was very nice about it — his choice of words was simple and direct.

"The governor has closed the state to fishing."

I looked into his eyes. "Why?"

"Because of the fires."

"What fires?"

"Those fires."

He turned and pointed — touché. But still, if I was going to go peaceably, I wasn't going to go without registering an objection, so I trotted out my best shot:

"Water doesn't burn."

Give the warden his due; he laughed and shook his head sympathetically, and together we waded back across the side channels like old friends ("Mister," he said, "You can't even step off the road and *pee* in Montana while the ban is on"). He had a bear trap trailered behind his jeep; the ranchers were complaining about grizzlies being chased out of the park by the flames.

"You can still fish Yellowstone," he said, when I asked him for advice. "The ban doesn't apply there."

Irony never knows when to quit. You could *fish* in Yellowstone Park, only you couldn't *drive* into Yellowstone
Park, all the entrance roads being closed. But again, it was a
matter of clinging to wisps now, literally and metaphorically, and so I decided to drive to West Yellowstone and wait
for some shifting pattern in the fires to give me my chance.

As I drove up the highway I saw the warden wading
through the river toward another fly-fisherman who cast all
unsuspecting upstream — set in the glorious riverscape, the
mirror image of what I had just been: a man a moment away
from heartbreak, flailing away at the sky with grace,
rhythm, and — dwarfed as he was by the rolling smoke
clouds — a small penumbra of the absurd.

West Yellowstone must be a tawdry enough place under
normal circumstances, filled as it is with vacant-eyed tourists
seeking to find in the garish streets that which escaped them
in the park, but in early September of 1988, with the fires
making headlines everywhere, the flames just a single block
away, it was against all probability one of the most interesting places in the world.

It's hard to do justice to that exaggerated, surrealistic
scene. The improvised, graffiti-like signs that met me as I
drove down Route 20 into town (*Welcome to Charcoal-
broiled National Park*); the line of yellow fire trucks lined
up ready to spring into action if the flames crossed the street
separating the village from the park; the lawn sprinklers
borrowed from every golf course in Montana, covering the
scrubby border zone with their arcing white spray; the
ghostlike emptiness of the motels; the heartbroken fishermen roaming about like me, absolutely at a loss; the legion
of green-panted, yellow-shirted fire fighters, the way they

crowded the restaurants and lined up at pay phones calling
home they were safe; the army jeeps swerving around corners on two wheels as if under fire; the way the T-shirt fac-
tories had switched gears and were churning out designs for
the current market (a fat grizzly picking his teeth with a
toothpick, saying "Who needs tourists? Send more firefight-
ers!"); the high-school football team running wind sprints
under falling ash as behind them the cheering squad prac-
ticed their splits. . . . It was a place under the gun, and like
all such places, it had gone more than a little bit nuts.

Seeing all this, seeing the school buses taking fresh fire
fighters into the park while other buses brought exhausted
ones out, smelling the smoke, seeing the huge, iodine-
colored cloud that kept expanding and moving closer (tending to a mushroom shape, but never quite taking it on), it
was impossible not to think of combat. The enemy was out
there in the hills, its whereabouts constantly shifting; there
were   retreats,   furious   counterattacks — communiqués
issued hourly for the reporters and TV crews camped in the
larger, luckier motels.

As with combat, it was impossible to get the story
straight. Everyone you talked to had a different rumor. The
town was going to be evacuated at eight that night; the town
was going to be evacuated at eight-thirty; the town was
going to be evacuated at nine, but only if the wind shifted
to the east. The forlorn fishermen gathered in the tackle
shops exchanged rumors of their own. It was going to snow
on Thursday and the season would be reopened; it was going
to snow on Thursday, but the season *wouldn't* be reopened;
it wasn't going to snow and the season wasn't going to be
reopened and the fires would never stop burning and all of
us might as well pack our fly rods and go home.

The strangest rumor concerned the West Entrance Road. Was it open or wasn't it? Some insisted yes, it was; others were equally adamant in saying no way. Since the West Entrance is approximately forty-five yards from the café in which this discussion took place, I decided — now that dinner was over — to walk past the sprinklers and take a look-see.

By some miracle it *was* open — the booths were manned by rangers just as on a normal day. The woman at the booth I stopped at didn't bat an eye when I asked for a fishing permit; she gave me the standard spiel about regulations, and before I quite realized what was happening, I was driving alone into the park along the Madison in a sunset that was starting a good three hours before it was due.

As it turned out, I didn't get very far. There in the opposite lane was a convoy of campers and cars being escorted out by rangers in jeeps; the scene, in the black-and-white haziness, reminded me of newsreels I'd seen of refugees fleeing the blitzkrieg in France. I still had no idea what they were doing letting people *in* at this time (I found out later the decision to open the West Entrance Road only lasted an hour or two); it was just one of those inexplicable windows of opportunity that open even in the messiest of wars. I drove about eight miles to the point where the land on either side of the road was blackened with smoldering embers, and there, open road or not, decided to stop.

I didn't go back right away; in fact, I did something I'm rather ashamed to admit: I put on my waders, tiptoed around the embers, let myself down into the cool Madison water, and began to fish.

West Yellowstone craziness had gone to my head. But irony, my nemesis, played a part, too. Having allowed me by a miracle into the park, it permitted me to advance only to a point on the Madison that was, I found out later, notorious for its absence of trout. I cast for an hour or more, pleased to have the river to myself, taking mental snapshots of the bizarre, otherworldly scene, only a little disappointed the fish weren't rewarding my foolhardiness with the appropriate bravos. By the time it was dark I realized something I'd been hiding from myself all along: that I wasn't enjoying myself — that with men and women being ferried in behind me to fight this awesome, unknown thing, fishing for trout seemed, as it never had before, the idle occupation of the vain.

There comes a point on any trip that is as much psychological as geographic when you've gone as far as you're going and everything else is simply return. That roadside pull-off eight miles inside a burning Yellowstone Park was that point for me. From then on in, my trip was only a kind of mopping-up exercise and I traveled without expecting much at all.

Still, I gave it one more try. When I woke up in the morning I drove south into Idaho toward the Henry's Fork, making what had been the obvious move all along. The fishing season was still open there — the rumors all agreed on that. That I had postponed going down there as long as I had was only due to my fear that every other disappointed angler in Montana would be doing exactly the same thing.

And that's pretty much how it turned out. I drove past campground after campground of troops getting ready for another day of fighting fires in the south part of the park. Crossing the state line, I stopped at Lee's Ferry for a license;

the man who sold it to me said he'd issued over a hundred on the previous afternoon.

I should have turned around right there. But I didn't — I drove to the "mailbox" just upstream of the famous Railroad Ranch, parked my car, suited up, then started the long hike into the river. It was a lovely morning, or at least it would have been if it wasn't for the smoke; if anything, it was even more biting and acrid than it had been farther north (and this was the day back in New York that people noticed an even stranger pall in the air than normal — the smoke from burning forests drifting eastward across the continent).

What's there to say about the Henry's Fork that hasn't been said before? It's beautiful water, set in a glorious vale, and once the sun warms the surface, the river comes alive with flies and rising trout. I didn't catch any, of course — no one actually *catches* a Henry's Fork trout. I took a certain amount of consolation in managing a rise or two. I took a great deal more consolation in seeing none of the other forty-three fishermen I could count from where I was standing catch one either.

Forty-three fishermen — the scene resembled a New Jersey trout stream on opening day. There were fishermen everywhere, not only wading, but riding along the riverbank on their dirt bikes, rods propped up on the handlebars like the bike-riding jousters in *A Connecticut Yankee in King Arthur's Court*. Every few yards they would pull over, put their kickstands down, hop into the river, cast, then climb back out and pedal on some more.

It was all rather interesting in its way. I hated it immensely.

I walked back to the car and drove toward Montana, my spirit pretty well broken. After a few miles I came to one of those places you see so often out West — a combination restaurant/motel/gas station/bar. I parked, went over to the phone booth, and in a few quick phrases made a reservation for a flight home the next day.

There didn't seem to be too much to do after that except eat lunch. At first, I was the only customer, but then three young fire fighters came in dressed in the green pants and soft yellow shirts I was beginning to envy. They were coming off the fire line for a reason I couldn't quite pick up; that they were tired and relieved was evident from their expressions. The two bearded ones were from Wyoming, and the thinner, slighter one, the one sitting across from them with eager, ash-ringed eyes, talking rapidly, was from somewhere in Utah.

"There's no turkey today," the waitress said, handing me a menu.

"Hamburger's fine," I said, handing it back.

To my left at the other table I heard the word *Jews*. I glanced around and saw it was the thin, beardless one who had said it. He was talking even faster now, caught up in his explanation.

"From Odessa, which is in the southern part of Russia. The Black Sea? That's where the Revolution began. Did you ever see the movie *The Battleship Potemkin?* They lived there and ran a shop that sold leather stuff. My grandparents. Do you know what a pogrom is?"

The huskier of the bearded men said he didn't know what a pogrom was.

"Mobs went around killing Jews and burning their homes. It had to do with rumors they spread about ritualistic killings. Jews were supposed to go around murdering children, and it was just an excuse to take their property. The czar encouraged it."

The waitress came back with my sandwich. "Pretty bad out there, huh?" I ventured.

"We're waiting on the wind," she said, with no inflection I could catch. "It blows from the east we're going to lose some stock. Already moved them twice."

"So they left," the young man said. "You know about the Lower East Side? In New York City?"

"We lost a mule back in July," the waitress said, wiping the hair back from her forehead. "Wandered too close to the fire, I guess."

"How did they get to Utah?" one of the bearded men asked.

"Tough," I said, shaking my head.

"They were afraid of cities. After the pogroms, all those walls. My grandfather wanted to live somewhere where there were no walls. No walls and lots of leather."

"Nobody tells us anything," the waitress said softly. "All we do is have to wait."

"Is a pogrom like the holocaust?" the second of the bearded men suddenly asked.

"I came out here to fish," I told her.

"Yeah," the thin one said, chewing away at his sandwich. "Like that."

"Tough," she said. "Pie?"

And so there we were, an odd enough quintet, the boys fresh back from fighting the apocalypse, talking in casual phrases of obscure destinies and ancient wrongs; the waitress with her stoic acceptance of tragedy that was just over the ridge now; me with my silly disappointment, a fisher of

the absurd glutted with his catch — the five of us slumped
there at the fag end of that summer of drought and ozone
depletion and global warming and a burning Yellowstone
Park.

The boys were still talking when I left. I envied them,
and not for their shirts this time, but for their youth — for
being immersed in the center of experience while I circled
the edges coughing in the smoke. But if nothing else, before
leaving I could get my belly full of that. I got in the car,
rolled the windows down so it would stream right in at me,
then headed north on the highway toward being forty after
all.

July 2

Morning swim, six-thirty A.M. The fog so thick I have to thrash through it just to find the shore of the pond. Lots of surprises emerge from that fog in the course of the summer. Snapping turtles laying their eggs, bitterns slipping through the marsh grass, raccoons tidying up the picnic area, once — miraculously — three lovely campers taking their morning baths. I make a point of coughing to warn whatever's *in* there I'm afoot, but this time the only thing that materializes is Cider, my golden, whose nose has taken her on an elliptical orbit from our car to the beach.

It's amazing how much moral credit I get for these morning swims — to hear people talk, you'd think I was flailing myself with ice. And yet there does come a time, stripping off my sweatshirt, coming skin to skin against the fog, that my every instinct is to turn around, run back to the car, and turn the heater on full blast. The fog is generated off the pond's surface so fast, with such turmoil, it creates its own damp breeze, so there's a reverse double shock in braving it — that first chilly plunge through the mist, followed by a warmer slap into the water.

So I always hesitate. If nothing else, it gives me time to check out the fishy population of the shallows. Trout, bass, contented sunfish. The pond contains them all, and there's almost always a troller out there making the rounds. Me, I prefer not to, even though it's the nearest body of water to my house. This is neutral territory in my conflict with the piscine kingdom, a buffer zone between my resolute pursuit and their resolute fleeing, a watery Switzerland where both of us can swim without worrying about who is or who isn't attached to whom.

And yet a fisherman has been at work here already — a blue heron who, seeing me now, lets out a deep, halfhearted squawk of protest, pulls its legs into its body, and flip-flops those lazy wings away into the fog. He's left his breakfast behind — a rock bass that lies spinning on its side in six inches of water, the body folded back on itself like a target that's been drilled.

A feeding heron, a dead rock bass — this is the pond's natural order at work. Still, coming upon death so suddenly on a morning so tranquil adds a deeper chill to the mist, and I hesitate there on the beach longer than usual, trying to get up the nerve to plunge through the various layers of vapory indecision and metaphysical doubt.

Deep breath, flapping of arms, stutter step, plunge, double plunge, stroke stroke stroke! There's nothing graceful about my entry, but all the splashing and yelling dissipates the fog just enough for the horizontal admittance of a man and his dog. Out I swim, rolling on my back to stretch the morning stiffness out, flopping back over and digging in freestyle, working myself gradually up to top speed. Cider, who has two speeds, mine and double mine, turns on the jets and disappears after some surface-skimming swallows, her jaws chomping open and closed like a crocodile's.

The swallows have nothing to worry about — they enjoy leading her on. In the meantime, I'm swimming in what I hope is the direction of the eastern shore, navigating between strokes by quick glances at the branches of a dead elm up on shore. The fog hides everything except that. After a while, I hardly know whether I'm swimming in water or air, the horizon is lost to me, and the fog muffles even the dipping sound of my hands as they reach, cup, and pull. With the body so disoriented, the mind retreats, too, until it hardly seems *me* swimming there at all; I'm off somewhere imagining all this, irritated at myself for dreaming up a waterscape so featureless and gray. Time to turn around before I bump into something — in this thick nebulosity, it's the only thought that coheres.

And then it happens.

I'm retracing my course, swimming through the trail of foam left by my kicks, when — my head rolling underwater — an all but imperceptible wave of pressure comes against my eyes and causes them to open. There three feet to my left and slightly deeper than the surface, moving on a parallel course to mine, is a flash of something gold. I say "flash" and "gold" as if my mind had time to register these things, shape the experience into words, but what really happened happened so fast it was over before I had time to blink. Still, re-creating it now, I remember the movement and gold coming to me in one sensory packet, like a sheaf of sunlit rays — how the gold seemed so bright and happy I wanted to fasten on to it the way a child at Christmas wants to grab an ornament off the tree . . . how my left hand reached from my normal stroke in a greedy, grabbing motion that came sweeping down toward the golden bauble, and — fluttering the shape of it — just barely missed.

These things — and how, missing, I felt both an ineffable sadness and a sudden fear. I rolled over and started treading water, gasping, all but shaking, just in time to make out, disappearing through the fog twenty yards ahead, the square stern of a fishing boat trolling the treble-hooked spinner for which I had grabbed.

A narrow miss then — my skin could all but feel those barbs sinking in. But there was as much disappointment in my reaction as there was fear, and it's only now I can make sense of it. That sudden appearance of color in the colorless element in which I swam; the tactile *definiteness* of it in my haze; the envy created by a speed that was greater than mine; the curiosity it engendered, the longing that was far more impulsive than any hunger; the nostalgic compulsion of that possessive juvenile response, *mine*. Here I'd been all season trying so hard to figure out my *why*, I'd forgotten the fish's *why*, and suddenly I had it, in a demonstration that could hardly have been clearer, more dangerous or plain.

What makes a fish take a lure?

I know now. For one fleeting moment the fog dissipates and I *know*.

Golden Age

Picture this for a golden age.

Trout that are widespread and plentiful, flourishing in waters that are perfectly suited to their rapid growth. A growing number of fly-fishermen with increased leisure time to pursue their avocation. The rapid development of lightweight tackle — new fly-rod designs that are much lighter and more powerful than anything seen so far; new and innovative fly patterns tied by fishermen with a deep understanding of aquatic life. A new conservation ethic that persuades even the lowliest trout-chaser he shouldn't keep all his catch, but must return some to ensure future propagation. Growing scientific interest in the species, with much that was left to hunch and instinct now being studied and described. A literature that celebrates the trout in all its splendor with a delightfully sweet lyricism that makes books on fly-fishing the proudest body of writing on any sport.

Picture all this, then try to give it a date. Eighteen

ninety-eight, when Henry Van Dyke was writing essays about little rivers and it was no trick at all for a beginning fly-fisherman to take fifty Catskill trout in a short afternoon? Nineteen ten, when Theodore Gordon and George M. L. La Branche were developing techniques and tactics so fundamental that they are still in use today? Certainly in our great-grandfathers' day, the glories far enough away now that they've taken on a bittersweet patina and shine through the years like the afterglow from an extinct Valhalla.

But the funny thing about golden ages is that you never realize you're in the middle of one until the gold turns to rust. Change a single word in the opening paragraph and you have, in every particular except one, a perfect description of the situation that applies today.

Change the word *trout* to *bass*.

It's a simple change, but one with wide significance. Fly-fishing for bass, so long the dowdy stepsister of fly-rodding for trout, is at last coming into its own. Next to me as I write is a catalog from a leading tackle house, and on its order blank are no less than fifty different fly and bug patterns tied exclusively for bass. Beside it is a recent issue of a fly-fishing magazine, with three articles on bass, each written at a high level of technical expertise. New graphite rods make casting bugs easier than it's ever been before, and tiers are creating flies that actually resemble what the bass eat. And while organizations like Trout Unlimited are doing wonders in preserving the trout's domain, the bass's range is scarcely threatened, and there are few places in this country where good largemouth or smallmouth fishing isn't available within a convenient drive.

But it is not what links these two golden ages that's important here, but what separates them. We have the fish and the tackle and the scientists, but there is one thing we don't have and it's a pity.

Where are the writers on bass?

I don't mean the lunker and hawg boys. There's a plague of these, God knows, each with their pet little theory to sell, each with their high-powered state-of-the-art user-friendly fishing reel and high-powered state-of-the-art user-friendly prose style. I mean instead the real writers, stylists who can compare with a Haig-Brown and Howard Walden from an earlier generation, or a Nick Lyons and Robert Traver from our own. It's not hard to make a list of people writing about bass with the same kind of originality, grace, and beauty these writers bring to bear on trout. The list begins and ends with a single digit: 0. The bass, for all its familiarity, is a noble fish, well deserving of a poet laureate, and instead it's held captive by a court of illiterate jesters tearing around in sinfully overpowered boats equipped with a thousand dollars worth of superfluous gear.

The absence of a bass literature to compare with the trout's has several reasons, some obvious, some not. The tradition from which American fly-rodding stems is a British tradition, of course, and British, too, are its literary anteced-ents, with Izaak Walton as patron saint. Thus, right from the start the poetic trout was deemed a proper literary sub-ject, while the humbler bass — unknown in England — was deemed, if not beneath contempt, at least beneath dignity.

Actually, bass fishing does have a patron saint, but he's a much different sort of man than Father Walton: Dr. James A. Henshall, M.D., he of the white walrus mustache and

silver pince-nez. I have the ninth edition of his classic *Book
of the Black Bass* in my collection — a beautiful copy, with
a golden smallmouth embossed on the cover, and above it
the famous motto that, like a catchy advertising jingle, made
the bass's reputation: *Inch for Inch and Pound for Pound,
the Gamest Fish that Swims.*

Henshall, writing at the turn of the century, makes no
pretense of his intentions. *"The Book of the Black Bass,"* he
writes in his introduction, "is of an entirely practical
nature. . . . It has been written more with a view to instruct
rather than amuse or entertain. The reader will, therefore,
look in vain between its covers for those rhetorical flights,
poetic descriptions, entertaining accounts and pleasing illustrations of the pleasures and vicissitudes of angling which
are usually found in works of like character."

So there we have it right from the start; Dr. Henshall
rules that for bass, poetry is out of bounds. It's a Philistin-
ism he doesn't always stick to — there are lovely passages
in the book where the good doctor quite forgets himself and
writes most lyrically — but for the main, he puts bass writing in the technical, how-to groove it remains in to this day.
Along with this, he launched that other annoying quality
that still infects so much bass writing: an obnoxious jingo-
ism; a boosterism designed as a corrective to the trout fisherman's disdain, but which in the end becomes so established
and ingrained it becomes a reverse snobbery of its own.

The Kentucky bait-casting reel didn't help matters either.
Its perfection (and the perfection of the spinning reel a few
decades later) pushed fly-fishing for bass to the periphery of
the sport, and widened the divergence between the English
lyric tradition and the new American technocratese. If the

best way to catch largemouth was to throw a one-ounce River Runt Spook at them, then the person doing the throwing was less apt to pick up a book of fly-casting recollections by, say, Lord Grey of Falloden, and more likely to pick up *Sports Afield* to see what Jason Lucus had to say about plug weights. Thus, the would-be bass writer had no Eugene Connets to emulate, no A. W. Millers. That bass fishing could be a beautiful experience, a balm and restorative to the soul, wasn't macho enough to be admitted; what counted in bass fishing, right through the plastic worm/tournament era, was horsing in those hawgs.

Even the bass's prolificacy worked against him. While the trout stylists cherished their fish all the more because he was so threatened, bass writers could wallow in their fish's abundance and afford all kinds of sloppiness, not only in their conservation ethic (or rather their lack of one), but in their prose. The catching of one trout became a ceremony to be celebrated, while with bass there was no use talking about it unless you came home with a full stringer. An individual trout was thought of as a miracle; an individual bass as a statistic, so there's no wonder someone with talent and sensitivity preferred writing about the former.

But if there are compelling reasons why bass writing has never produced its *A River Runs Through It* or its *Upstream and Down* in the past, there is no reason why it may not do so in the future. For there are signs of hope. Fly-fishing for bass is undergoing a tremendous resurgence of interest, as witnessed by all those new fly patterns, all those new tactics. Some of our best fishermen are beginning to realize that not only is fly-rodding a good way of taking bass, at some times and at certain places it's the *best* way. Every year around the first week of July, I have the same conversation at a boat landing near my home on the Connecticut River. A jump-suited bass man will trailer out his souped-up Ranger and allow as to how he's given up for the year, since the bass have gone deep where he can't get at them, even with his fish finder. I smile at this. All summer the smallmouth will be rising freely to bugs along the shore, and the finest sur-face fishing of the year is only just starting as the plastic-tossers give up.

The resurgent popularity of bass bugging is bound to result in new writing that comes from the fly-fisher's unique perspective — that is, from a perspective that combines pro-found curiosity with deep respect. The new breed of bass writer will not be afraid to give us those "rhetorical flights, poetic descriptions" and "entertaining accounts" that Dr. Henshall so disdained — will instead glory in them and so produce a body of bass-fishing literature that can stand proudly against our best, most lyrical writing on trout.

What kind of literature will this be? I'm playing hunches now, but they're strong ones. It will be a literature with a remarkable geographic range, taking in not only glacial lakes in Maine and farm ponds in Indiana but swamps in the Lou-isiana bayou country and man-made impoundments in the Nevada desert. It will be a literature set on still water more than rivers, plains more than mountains, with perspectives that are those of expanse. It will be an aural literature, splashy with sounds. It will be a literature that is tangential, full of anecdotes; things *happen* in bass fishing, crazy things that aren't necessarily connected to the fishing. It will be a literature that is nostalgic for a simpler era without being maudlin — a literature that treats with respect the old wooden plugs and sparrow-sized bass bugs and boats that had to be rowed. It will be an extroverted literature, the focus being on the other fishermen in the boat rather than on the fisherman telling the tale. It will be, above all, a literature that is as pugnacious and brave as the bass itself, one that comes at you with unexpected leaps and cantankerous little flourishes and a great unquenchable tug of joy.

I think of the bass writing to come, and I think of two evenings last August when I fished a small mountain lake on the height of land behind my home. It's a clear, stony lake of the kind found in northern New England, complete with its resident loons and its osprey and its deer coming down to shore at sunset for a curious stare about. There are smallmouth in it, few very big, but possessed of a brightness and energy that do ample justice to the beauty of the scene.

Near the eastern shore is an old logging dam, and from its base extends a vast shallows of boulders dark and craggy enough to gladden the heart of a Robert Frost. I was in a canoe on that first night; for reasons I'm not sure of, I'd brought along a spinning rod with a tackle box full of ancient Bass o'Renos and rusty Jitterbugs I'd used as a boy.

About seven, just as the sun touched the mountain's shoulder on the lake's far shore, smallmouth started rising on all sides, so that within seconds the surface that had been completely placid was dimpled with interconnected, outspreading rings. The effect was that of a rainstorm with no rain — I held my palm out, expecting to feel drops. As it turned out, the bass were rising to a small white mayfly I'd never seen before, and totally ignored my meatier plug. Some were leaping free of the surface and not just sipping; there was something so startling and unexpected in the explosive way they shot clear, yet so fixed and regular in the parabola described by their reentry, that I began thinking of summer fireworks and not summer rain.

I was back the following night, this time with my fly rod and some small white Irresistibles that perfectly imitated the hatch. By the time I actually saw a fish jump it was too late to cast to him, but if I kept my line in the air and waited, I'd notice a rise a few feet away, and by dropping the line a few feet from *that* I could anticipate the bass's direction and so have him.

It was fishing of the most exciting and yet gentlest sort, and by the time it became too dark to see, the pattern of the catching had become mixed with the whistly gargle of the loons and the humming crickets back in the beaver swamps and the steady lap of water against the canoe's bow, so that it seemed I was reeling these in, too, and not just fish.

Thirty bass, thirty-five. I don't remember how many I caught and it's not important. What is was that sense of levitation — the feeling that all the smallmouth in the lake were devoting themselves that night to pushing the already airy surface even higher, so that the whole experience, myself included, floated a foot above the real lake in a magic realm where anything might happen.

That was your golden age for you, right down to the sunset, which — touching the far shore now — sent a ripple across the lake that transformed itself halfway across from a ray of magenta light to a pulse of cool wind that shivered me in absolute delight.

July 24

There's luck and there's *luck.*

A simple illustration. We're lucky to live a short drive from the picture-perfect village of Strafford, Vermont. Set in a valley where the fields are cleared and open in the old way, its dwellings little changed in appearance since the Civil War, the village boasts what my editor friend Tom Slayton likes to call the Chartres of Vermont — the immaculate white meetinghouse set high above the west side of the common. It also boasts, a short way down the common, one of the best bike-repair shops in New England. Me being the avid bike rider and mechanical illiterate I am, I'm lucky in this proximity.

The shop's proprietor is a multitalented, sophisticated man whose world encompasses a lot more than ten-speeders. Among other things, he's a devoted bird hunter, and I always make a point of asking him how the shooting's been while he prods and pokes my gears. He tells me a hunting story or two, I lie about the fishing, and the conversation is, I like to think, conducted on a plane of mutual curiosity and respect worthy of Piscator and Venator in Izaak Walton.

We're lucky to have a man like that around. As I was leaving his shop one day, Richard — who never loses faith in one's ability to surmount one's mechanical deficiencies — yelled after me this advice: "Try fixing that yourself next time! All you need is a number-eleven wrench!"

Right. But the advice was generously offered, and I filed it away in the list of things I must do someday. I drove the dozen miles home, parked my car near the village common, cut across the grass toward the general store, felt something hard crunch below my shoe, bent down, and discovered there in the grass a wrench — a wrench that, when I lifted it and brushed off the dirt, had the number *11* engraved on its stem.

That's *luck*.

Of course, there's bad luck, too, but even this has a way of turning in unexpectedly happy directions. This afternoon I managed to clear my desk off early and drive up to the Waits after too many days away. I went in by the cemetery stretch, waved on my way by the cheerful red-bearded farmer who works the adjacent farm — seeing me, he likes to hold his hands apart, tilt his head in a question mark, and laugh. This stretch of river is set well below the road and pretty much ignored, but since it's the upper limit of brown trout range, the lower limit of brookies, it's fun discovering which ones are currently in residence.

The brookies as it turned out. On my first cast a decent ten-incher took my Royal Wulff in the pocket along a fallen, water-scoured maple. I landed him quickly, released him into the current, and was heading upstream to the next pool when my wading shoes came against a mossy rock and I slipped. Slipped, not fell; in fact, it was hardly even a "slip" more than a quick readjustment in my posture from slightly tilted to fully upright. Unluckily, what tilted the most was the hand carrying my new Orvis graphite fly rod. The butt came down on the table-sized boulder next to me, and then, with a plastic sighing, separated out into its approximately 130 constituent strands.

Strands that, luckily enough, hadn't been severed. Always before when I've broken a rod, it's been at the ferrule where the break is dramatically complete. This time the filaments, separated on the latitudinal plane, were still connected on the longitudinal one; it was as if the rod had transformed itself into an eight-and-a-half-foot assemblage of black spaghetti. That it was three hundred dollars down the tubes bothered me, of course; what hurt even more was that, weaponless, my fishing trip was prematurely over.

So, alternatives time. Cast by hand? I've seen it done, casters whipping out line as dexterously as Indiana Jones, but only as a stunt. Not fish at all, wade upstream, do some "research"? Good idea in theory, but a fly-fisherman without a fly rod is like a microbe hunter without a microscope, and it's my fixed belief that it is only *through* the delicate intermediary of the fly rod that we really focus our attention on a stream's life.

There was another alternative, the one I went for. Up in my glove compartment was some electrician's tape used to patch some earlier victim of my clumsiness. I tore off a piece, wound it as tight as I could from the grip to the ferrule, waved the mended rod back and forth in a mock cast, then took it back down to the river hoping for the best.

It cast. It didn't cast pretty and it didn't cast far, but it cast. That was the lucky part. The *unlucky* part was that when I rose the next trout, the response time — the time it took my upward-lifting impulse to be transmitted through the tape to what was left of the fiber — was so slow the fish was long gone by the time the line tightened. The same thing happened on the next pool upstream: another good fish, another slow-motion miss.

Well, I was *almost* there. What I needed besides the tape was a splint of some kind, something that would add rigidity — a branch, say. The moment I brought my head down to look for one — the very moment! — I saw something long and cream-colored on the bank: a kid's fiberglass fishing rod, the cheap kind that costs a few bucks in the five and ten, abandoned there who knows when, absolutely perfect — when broken in half — for my splints.

It was the work of a few seconds to unwrap the tape from my rod, graft in the added section of the kid's, and wrap the bastardized hybrid back up. I tried a cast, and the action seemed much stiffer than before, much faster. I waded up to the next pool, worked out as much line as I dared, and — holding my breath the entire time — hooked and landed a twelve-inch trout, the nicest brookie I'd taken all summer.

That's *luck*.

But even then it wasn't finished. If you fish the Waits much you'll hear stories about an eighty-year-old woman who divides her time between tending a tag-sale table outside her simple home and fishing the river every night just long enough to catch dinner for her cat. I'd heard about her from several sources, and though I'd kept my eyes open, six years had gone by and I'd never actually seen the fish lady in person.

I don't have to tell you what happened. Driving home that night, trying to decide if it was my unlucky day because of breaking the rod or my lucky day because of mending it, I saw a movement in the twilight near the river's edge . . . pulled the car over . . . and saw emerge from the alders a little stooped-over woman carrying a spin-casting rod, a worm bucket, two long trout, and — trotting behind at a respectful distance — a smug-looking Siamese cat.

I could all but feel the scale tip — LUCKY. Getting home late, I rushed right out to the barn and rubbed the totem responsible there in its bracket above the paint: my beautiful, well-tempered number-eleven wrench.

A River of a Certain Age

In shaking a life loose from the trivia of daily routine, airing it out in the open where there's a chance for perspective, there are at least two approaches. The first is to appraise everything you do with the eye of the twelve-year-old that lurks in each one of us, delight him or her by the actual immersion in an experience that as a child was only dreamed. The other is to look at that same experience from the opposite angle, from the old person we will all too soon become, and from that perspective savor every experience for the fleeting moment it really is. At forty, you're torn between both approaches — rewarding the kid in you for all that wanting; consoling the old man in you for all those regrets.

Because I realize this — because, forty myself now, I can begin to sense the shadows cast by even the most commonplace events — I have a hunch there are certain experiences that better be stored in memory right. Moments of love, moments of labor, moments of fun. Part of the delight in these has always been to think of my twelve-year-old self romping in an adult world of endless possibility, but increasingly, with this new prescience, I find the pleasure is apt to come from that other focus, of thinking how good this will all be summoned back in leisurely remembrance.

And so in the store of these last, knowing I'll need it, I would like to enter the following: a hot and sunny mid-June afternoon in any of the years 1982–90. I've spent the morning writing and managed to finish something I've struggled over for weeks. Now, with the long afternoon ahead of me, I'm sliding my green fifteen-foot Old Town Acadia canoe (remembrance delighting in specificity!) into a lazy-flowing river a short distance from my home. Into the canoe goes an extra paddle in case I drop one; a thermos full of cranberry juice; a frozen bottle of Guinness lager; a bag of ham and cheese sandwiches; an eight-and-a-half-foot graphite Orvis fly rod; an old Almaden wine box filled with extra bugs, flies, streamers, and leaders; and — most important of all for a redhead — a six-ounce container of number-twenty-eight Johnson & Johnson sunscreen.

And yes — myself, dressed in the khaki-colored pith helmet that makes my friends kid me about safaris, orange sneakers still damp from the last time I made this trip, and green hospital scrubs I was given the morning I was coaching Celeste in labor, and — coaching aggressively — my pants split down their seams.

Everything loaded? Fine, off I go. The water — cobalt and mysterious in the center of the river, startlingly clear in the six-foot-wide fringe along the banks — is flowing downstream at a slow but perceptible pace, the gates being open at the dam fifteen miles below. I see the motion first in the

way the pale green weeds off the boat landing stream in that
direction, then feel it as the canoe comes fully out into the
current and takes on motion itself; the effect, in water so
otherwise tranquil, is like stepping out onto a moving sidewalk that frees you of any obligation but to keep to the right
and glide.

Motion first, then smells. Manure up on the banks — I
look up to see some Holsteins tranquilly crapping as this
horizontal apparition sails past. Honeysuckle blossoms
lower down — a sweet wild smell that seems broadcast and
exaggerated by the heat of the sandy banks. New-cut hay,
an old favorite — in a field on the far shore a red tractor
finishes its sweep and turns in a wide circle around. A water
smell that's not of water at all, but of earth carried down
from the tributaries upstream, held in suspension, so that
the whole river, in an olfactory sense, seems an enormously
long furrow turned in warm and fragrant soil.

When motion and smells drop into place — a hundred
yards from where I started — I touch the paddle long
enough to make the canoe drift closer to shore, then, like a
man reaching out to measure familiar boundaries, I work out
my line in a first cast. There are trees in the water here, old
spruce that crashed from the bank in the high water of
spring, and from the complicated archipelago of bark formed
by their branches a silver twenty-inch pike comes up to
devour my Sneaky Pete popper. He fights wildly, bizarrely,
fleeing out into the river *away* from safety, and for a change
the leader doesn't snap in his teeth and I manage to carefully
land and defeather him. Beyond, in a smaller tree, is a monstrous rock bass, a brute of a sunfish, and a cast beyond him
is a fat bluegill sunbathing above a sandbar, and here it is

ten minutes since I left and I already have three good fish
and I haven't even started trying for the species I've come
for.

They're over on the New Hampshire shore where the
banks become both steeper and rockier. I have one on almost
immediately, then a second and a third — smallmouth bass,
absolutely frantic with energy, and they prance and splash
and dive like contestants in a swim meet whose winner
depends upon my scoring. Bass by the mile — there's no
end to them! — and they're in tight a few inches from shore
where the overhang of branches makes the taking of them
require just enough preciseness to make it interesting; preciseness, and yet the casts that bring fish fastest are the bad
ones that rebound off the leaves into the water like vertigi-
nous bugs.

The rocks give way to sandier, more barren stretches, but
it's no trick at all to paddle a few times on the left and let
the current glide me back over to Vermont. There are all
kinds of rocks here — the Boston and Maine railroad tracks
run right along the river — and basses twenty, twenty-one,
and twenty-two are quickly hooked, fought, boated, and
released. I'd like to think there are differences between New
Hampshire bass and their Vermont cousins, the latter being
less reactionary, more generous and fair, but they refuse to
fit my political anthropomorphism, and fight with matching
splendor, free of any cant.

A pause now — a low, barely perceptible disturbance in
the river makes me think a beaver is about, but then the
sound loses its liquid quality and becomes established as a
definite rumble in the embankment to my right. A freight
train approaches from the south, chugging slowly up the

tracks with the cautious side-to-side wobble a dinosaur might display returning from extinction. I have a bass on, and with a little upward nudge from my rod he obliges with a jump just as the engineer leans out of the locomotive and waves. The engineer — God bless him! — blows his horn in salute, and between the vibration of the rocks and the shadows of the boxcars and the lonely hoot of the horn, the bass, train freaks all, really go nuts, so for many yards it becomes literally impossible to retrieve the popper without having a strike.

There's a cliché about catching so many fish your arm starts to ache, but it's no cliché because my forearm throbs now like I've played six sets of tennis, and I pull over into an eddy below some spruce to recuperate over lunch. When I'm trout fishing I eat abstemiously (like Cyrano de Bergerac, a grape and a macaroon), but when I'm bass fishing I like to wallow in all the fat and alcohol I can stand — for me, a piece of strawberry cheesecake and a single twelve-ounce beer. Finishing, I take a walk along the shallows near shore. The river mud is slick and treacherous, peppered with raccoon tracks, but it's cool on my bare feet, and above me the blue spruce shadows shimmy back and forth like fans.

The afternoon is much the same. More bass, more sunshine, more of that lush, pastoral landscape with which this valley is endowed. Six hours go by and I don't see another boat or another person, not even up on shore. This beautiful river, the splendid fish, and no one has caught on yet, not a single person! After a while it doesn't seem I'm drifting in a canoe at all, but riding the crest of a blossoming something, being lifted up by the life force's outspreading petal, and not a life force that's abstract, but one comprised of those leaping bass and darting swallows and the warmth exuded from the river's center. The feeling impresses itself so deeply — the feeling of abundance, of being able to dip my hands into a well of anything I want, fish, flowers, farmland, and sky — that it stays with me long after I leave the river, so for the entire night I feel gliding, uplifted, *borne*.

All these things, and then, with a long paddle home ahead of me, the breeze switches direction and blows my canoe back upstream with the effortless, stately propulsion of an emperor's barge.

The river I'm talking about here, the ribbon of experience that ties these memories together, is the Connecticut — the longest river in New England, and, on a June day like this one, the prettiest. Starting hard by the Quebec line in a pond hardly bigger than its name, Fourth Connecticut Lake, it flows south nearly three hundred miles through four states to the whitecaps and sandbars at its mouth in Long Island Sound. For most of its course the width stays remarkably constant — the width, to compare fair to foul, of a four-lane interstate highway complete with shoulders and median. And while narrow in one sense, the river is absolutely central, drawing upon a watershed that takes in well over half of New England. You can see this best from the air. Every intersecting valley from Canada south, every parallel hill, every ridge and fold, furrow and trickle, seems to have as its purpose one goal and one goal alone: to support and nourish the low silver line looping back and forth at its center.

So essential is the river to this region that whatever allegiance local people seem to have to a "place" is to what is called the "Upper Valley" — that corridor extending from Windsor-Claremont an indefinite distance upstream. There's much logic in this — a watershed forms a better natural division than a state, and people hereabouts have much more in common with Vermonters across the river than they do with people living beyond the hills in Concord, the state capital. And while valley dwellers can be susceptible to narrowness of focus, they seem increasingly willing to acknowledge a basic truth: that we live upstream of neighbors and downstream of neighbors and in this day of environmental interdependence, we're all in one valley together.

Just as the Connecticut is central to this region, it's central to our town, even though few who live here seem aware of the fact. The village itself is set a mile east of the river where its plain meets the first big hills; the town owns no land on the riverbank, there is no place to launch a boat, and it's my guess that the majority of townspeople have never ventured out onto its water even once in their lives. This includes our local fishermen. They will spend hour after hour trolling circles around our swimming pond for hatchery trout, while only a short distance away is one of the best wild-bass fisheries in New England, which is almost totally ignored.

This seems exactly opposite to how things should be. Meeting a neighbor casually on the common I'm tempted to begin every conversation with the query "How's the river today?" — make a ritual acknowledgment of its presence. Even apart from the fishing it forms the best wildlife habitat in town, though people hereabouts, for all the lip service they pay to "country" life, are too suburbanized in outlook to care much about that. When the town does notice the river it's usually to destroy it; there was a grassy knoll at the mouth of a tributary where fathers would take their kids fishing, but our local developer has seen fit to build himself a boathouse there, a monstrosity straight out of Disney World, and so the families can't go there anymore and another bit of riverine beauty is chipped maliciously away.

The town did not always ignore the Connecticut this way. In the years when the fields were all cleared many of the farmers would have been along the banks for the better part of a working day, and a good proportion of men and boys worked during the winter rolling logs onto the frozen river from cuttings up in the hills. There are pictures of crowds lining the bank in the spring to watch the log drives, which must have been the great event of the year. One picture shows them on the North Thetford Bridge (swept out in the ruinous 1936 flood, so only the classic stonework of its supports now remains), peering down in happy curiosity at some bedraggled river men standing wearily amid a logjam with their cant dogs and pikes.

The bridges were private in those days, crossed by paying a toll, and there's a story they tell from Civil War days about the town contingent of 16th New Hampshire volunteers marching away with a splendid send-off toward the railroad station across the river in Vermont. When they got to the toll bridge, the collector — a true Yankee — wouldn't let them cross until they paid their toll, thereby putting things like patriotism and martial glory in their proper place.

The last log drive was in 1927, and it's been years since the river was worked here. Upstream by the paper mill in Groveton you can still see traces of what it was like heavily used — tawdry and nondescript — and it's these mills starting at Saint Johnsbury that explain in part why our town has so relentlessly turned its back on its essential geographic fact. Pollution — the filth that once made cynics call the Connecticut "the most beautifully landscaped sewer in the world."

There's an irony here — thanks to the heroic labors of river advocates, the Connecticut is being cleaned up. But the cleaner it gets, the more people find their way to its water, and what was once spoiled by sewage now becomes spoiled by fleets of powerboats and homes built too close to the banks. It's the familiar American paradox — neglect or crush, neglect or crush, with no possibility of a sensible in-between.

I've strayed a long way from that perfect June afternoon. But it's one of the characteristics of big rivers that anything puny tends to get swamped, and I suppose measured against the weight of those 250 miles, all the dreams and defeats of the human landscape through which this water runs, my own moment of quiet enjoyment forms barely a molecule. Rivers flow two ways, at least the big ones, and even here in rural New Hampshire the Connecticut carries the sense of Springfield's concrete and Hartford's sprawl and all the various forms of ugliness and indifference to be found from here to the river's mouth.

Big river. I can all but hear the snort of contempt from those who know really big rivers — in Mississippi terms, the Connecticut is an irrigation ditch for watering the cows. But there are other ways for a river to be big besides size — big in history, big in spirit — and in these measures, the Connecticut, New England's locus, has always been world-class.

And even if it wasn't, in my mind, on my own personal

scale of river size, the Connecticut would still rank as big, and for a reason I'm reluctant to admit: I'm afraid of it. In the narcotic lull of that perfect June afternoon, fishing late on moonlit summer nights, casting for bass in September's bayoulike fog. Nine tenths of me is aware of nothing but sheer joy in being out there, but that last tenth, the wary, too-imaginative tenth, is vaguely waiting for the river to pounce.

There, I've said it: big rivers are the ones that make us scared. Part of me is afraid of the Connecticut, though I'm not even sure what it is that makes me feel this way. There are objective dangers of a kind here. The dam down at Wilder backs up the river a distance of forty miles into a long and very narrow lake; unlike most lakes, there is no gradual drop-off from shore — six feet out, you're in water over your head. Deep, the river stays colder longer into spring, so even in June a capsize can spell trouble. Not too long ago a canoe was found floating empty here, it's owner, a champion white-water racer, discovered drowned a good distance downstream. Similar things are always happening — the Connecticut seems to have the evil knack of taking the young, gifted, and strong.

What's more, the Connecticut *looks* dangerous, at least up close. There are logs in the water, the heavy business ends two-thirds submerged in the sardonic manner of alligators and icebergs; chunks of collapsed bank with those bad-looking sweepers; weed beds whose strands are so long and oddly tropical they could be the abode of man-eating clams; enough pollution, on rainy days, to turn the river a shade too brown. Added to these is a haunted quality that gives the sensation you get on a man-made lake created over an abandoned village — the sense you're floating over a vanished epoch and can all but hear the ancient fiddles tuning up for a ghostly dance. Rural self-sufficiency, pastoral isolation. What was here is no longer and never will be again — the Connecticut knows this, and there's something resonant in the riverscape that can send a frisson of regret down the neck of even the dullest.

But I think in the end what my fear stems from is the reading of another message the river is constantly doing its best to transmit: that harnessed and tamed as it is, reduced from its wild glory, a Samson in chains, it still aches to burst loose from its channel, regain its freedom, destroy the dams, and until the day that happens, it will erode a bit, haunt a little, wreak its vengeance on one unfortunate canoeist at a time.

The Connecticut, then, is a channel of secret beauty running through the plain of everyday — a suggestive layer of remembrance superimposed over our amnesic age. The exploration of its riches should be enough to fill up the leisure hours of even a nonintrospective man, and yet in my case — God forgive me! — it is not. Like a boy reaching into a cereal box for the toy at the bottom, I ask more from the Connecticut than just the spiritual nourishment that comes with silence, scenery, and space: I want, want even desperately, a prize.

Smallmouth bass. It's their inhabitance that fascinates me, their pursuit that lures me out. The river is full of them here, fish that take on the same green-gold darkness as the water, so you can say of them what Thoreau said of Walden's pickerel, that they seem the "animal *nuclei*" of the river — Connecticut "all over and all through." Not large in the average, they more than make up for it with the spirit in which they fight. We're talking strong fish here, wild fish, and they react to the curtailment of their liberty with more instinctive rebellion than almost any creature that exists. Their huge indiscriminate mouths (smallmouth is only a relative term), the flexible armor of their gills, their squat full-back bodies, and the muscular spring of their hurdler's tails — these are fish that are superbly equipped to eat, run, and jump, and to be fastened to one for even a few seconds is to feel plugged into the life force at its maximum voltage.

When I moved here I was slow to find out just how good the bass fishing was. There were trout streams to fish, ponds to explore, and it wasn't until my third summer that I began trying to understand what the Connecticut was all about. Even then, I did most of my early fishing with spinning tackle and plugs, and I soon got bored with the assembly-line monotony of that kind of fishing. It was only when a friend gave me a fly rod heavy enough for serious bugging and a tackle box crammed full of poppers that I began to find the proper methodology — began to see how the disciplined ethic of fly-fishing I'd managed to teach myself over twenty years of chasing trout could be expanded to take in this new kind of river, this different kind of fish. Spin casting is casting *at* a fish, but fly casting is casting *to* them, and the difference, small as it sounds, is enough to elevate a recreation into a craft.

The fly rod is an epistemological tool the wielding of which gains us entry into a river's life — this is just as true on a slow-moving bass river as it is on a freestone stream. On the latter, with long experience and if things go right, fly-fishing can give you the feeling that every secret in the river is potentially graspable, all it takes is a little more care, a little more sharpness. On big rivers like the Connecticut, the knowing is much more tentative; with our casts covering so small a proportion of the total water, it's like chipping away at a secret with a chisel. And while bass fishing is invariably compared to trout fishing without either being particularly illuminated, I find the two fishings, these two ways of knowing, complement each other perfectly. There is a quality to trout fishing that doesn't bother me while I'm at it, but which I become aware of when I'm fishing for something else — something cramped in it all, the necessarily small scale (at least here in New England) of fish and river size, and the corresponding mind-set of fitting ourselves into something thus circumscribed. On the Connecticut, with no trees to entangle backcasts, with the views extending far in every direction, with the potential, especially in the backwaters, for seriously large fish, I'm aware of being released somehow — of exercising that part of me that finds joy in expansion, power, and force. Anyone who alternates between freshwater and saltwater fishing will know what I'm talking about here — how refreshing it can be after delicate casting to put all your strength into a powerful rod and really start to *haul*.

Sloppiness comes as a relief at times, in fishing just as in life. River bass are earthy fish, generously forgiving, and if you have the time and place down right, they will overlook a certain exuberance in your method. Here in the Connecticut their abundance is such that you're almost certain to find one who's in the mood for whichever fly you're using, be it a swallow-sized Dhalberg Diver, a moth-sized Bass King, or a streamer with eight inches of marabou trailing backward over the shank. There are just enough contaminants in the water (as if I'm praising them!) that people are reluctant to eat their fish, and so release them; with this, the coolness of the water, and the extensive cover, catches of twenty-five or thirty bass are common, at least in early summer. By August they're lazier, but bigger, and there always seems to be a spurt in September when the largest fish of the year become susceptible to yellow Woolly Worms jigged close to shore. But this is only a general trend. There are days even in August when some trick of rain or temperature will produce daytime fishing every bit as fast and exciting as June's.

The Connecticut, generous as it is, has certain peculiarities as a bass fishery, and anyone fishing my stretch of river will have to come to terms with these before getting into the heavy catches. Backed up by the dam as it is, with the drop-off so sudden, the fish hang in tighter to shore than any fish in any water I know. The cover is there — the bankside rocks and protective blowdowns — and between these, the availability of crayfish on the sandy bottom, the insects falling off the overhanging trees, the relative warmth of the sunny "shallows," the nearness of deep-water safety, you get a fishery that, in essence, isn't much wider than a small mountain brook. Many times, in fishing this strip, I've had the uncanny feeling I wasn't fishing water at all, but dry land. One of the most effective casts is to drop your popper on the rocky shingle, then pull it abruptly into the water. Six inches from shore may mean water two feet deep, and the bass, with excellent visibility, will often take the fly before it travels even a millimeter farther. How *far* they will come is something that varies tremendously from week to week; early in the season they seem to shy away from leaving the bank at all, but later in the summer they will often trail a lure ten yards and more, and the biggest have the trick of taking just as you're starting your next cast.

There are other peculiarities. Unlike the bass lakes only a few miles away, Connecticut fishing seems to improve in direct proportion to the thermometer, so the hotter it gets the faster the bass feed. This has it limits, of course. We had a heat wave last year that was either one of those unpredictable bumps in the weather pattern or a foretaste of what global warming will do to our summers. In either case, it pretty much put an end to the fishing by early July. But in most years the hot weather brings the fish up, particularly at the beginning of a season or the finish. Conversely, a cold front is enough to spoil the fishing for a day or two; on those crisp, invigorating days of northwest wind, I leave my canoe on the lawn and head for a trout stream instead, finding — after all that wide-open athleticism — the delicate preciseness to be just what I need.

There's the weather to take into account, and there's the tide — the daily rise and fall of the water level as the gates are opened at Wilder Dam fifteen miles to the south. The usual pattern is for the river to be at its highest in the morning, then to start dropping as the power demand peaks with the heat of the afternoon, rising again in the evening. Depending on the weather, the range can be extreme; I've seen mornings when the river seemed an inch from flooding over its banks, afternoons when there were mud flats along shore littered with sunburnt crayfish. And while I've spent many hours trying to find the link between these fluctuations and the fishing, I've never come to any conclusions I have much faith in. Is the fishing best when the water level is highest, offering more cover? Not particularly. Is it better at dead low, when the fish have fewer places to hide? No, I don't think so. If anything, it seems best at slack tide — the water neither too high nor too low, with perhaps just a suggestion of a downstream current.

Lures? I'm tempted to say any standard bass popper will do, but there's one so superior it deserves special mention: the chartreuse Sneaky Pete. Small and bullet-shaped, with long spidery legs and a pert, feathery tail, it takes more and bigger bass than any other lure I've tried ("Did you catch them on Sneaky Pete, Daddy?" my three-year-old daughter will ask the moment I come home). What's more, it casts well, not like those heavy bass bugs that make you feel, hauling it out there, that you and your lure are traveling in different time zones. You could fish exclusively with Sneaky up on top, pack along a few Woolly Buggers or Zonkers for times when they're deep, and be set for anything.

But careful here. Whenever I start to offer advice this way I feel the same flush of arrogant guilt I experience whenever I talk about technique in fiction — as if anyone can take something so magical and reduce it to formulas! There are general parameters for bass fishing, hunches and intuitions, but no rules. And whereas in trout fishing the tactics are so complicated and structured that for many fishermen method serves as its own reward, in bass fishing a much more pragmatic ethic is at work: the goal is to get out there and get some fish.

And what fish! Much more delicate than their lake-dwelling cousins, they have the knack of sipping in a popper so quietly you'd swear it was being attacked by a bubble — delicately, but once the line tightens all hell breaks loose, as if by some thermal bassy reaction their fastidiousness has been transformed into sheer bravado. Up they go exploding from the water, then submarining down into the depths, then skyrocketing upward again, this time out on the other side of the canoe, *kapowie!* . . . Well, as you can see, it's practically impossible to write about smallmouth without falling into a pinball-machine, italicized kind of prose (just as it's impossible to talk about them without wiggling your hand back and forth like a Spitfire pilot at a debriefing). They deserve better from a writer, much more lyricism and grace, and my literary resolution holds fast until I have one on the end of my line again, and then . . . *Zap! Zap! Powie!* Up they go! It's a great fish to catch on a fly rod, but a lot harder one to capture in prose.

It's odd to think how many of the happiest moments of my life, literally the happiest, have been spent chasing these feisty little bombshells with the squat, take-it-or-leave-it kind of name. The time I took my father out on the river one morning shortly after the birth of his granddaughter; how instead of our usual skunking we caught fish after fish, and my father's face lit up in surprise, wonder, and delight. Celeste and I out in *Bismarck*, our toy inflatable boat; how we caught not bass but one of those fringe benefits you often come across in pursuing bass, a walleye, a big four-pounder that towed us a good hundred yards along shore. Celeste again, this time reeling in a perch only to have a monstrous pike appear from the weeds to sever it in two. Owls, a whole parliament of them, barn, screech, and short-eared, twisting their necks around to watch us at twilight until you'd swear they were about to come unscrewed. All the flotsam and jetsam the river carries, finding among the half-submerged cornstalks Frisbees of all sizes and lollipop colors; Frisbees from new pizza shops opening in villages upstream, Frisbees left behind after river picnics, Frisbees lost in the water by teary-eyed kids — a whole river of Frisbees! The covered bridge at Clay Brook; how one July evening fishing alone in the endless dusk, I thought of writing a short story about a fourteen-year-old boy who must choose between the girl of his longing and the bass of his dreams. All these things, and where did they come from? The intense delight I find in spending a few seconds attached to a smallmouth bass.

We started out on the river this trip, stayed there for the most part, and we'll soon finish where we began — there in the sunlight catching fish. In a fraternal way I hope I've explained, the Connecticut has been my silent partner in these episodes, so when I come home at night it's not with the feeling that an "I" has caught these experiences, but this much more essential, satisfying "we."

Me and the Connecticut, brothers unto death. It's the kind of feeling a big river leaves in you, the endless downstream flow of it being such an obvious metaphor for time's own inevitable rhythm. Here in New England this note is played even more explicitly than it is elsewhere. Thinking back on its history, remembering the Puritans who settled here with their burden of piety and guilt, it's hard not to picture New England being born old, and living through the centuries, not toward senescence but toward a much delayed and much welcome youth.

And maybe this explains the fellow feeling — that here at the end of the Twentieth Century, the Connecticut River has at last reached a mature middle age, and so it's no wonder I identify with its complicated intermingling of freshness and hope, pollution and neglect — those alterations between

wild surges of energy and lazier, more introspective drift-
ings. *Old Man*, Faulkner called the Mississippi, but it's different on the Connecticut, and if either of us, river or man,
is headed toward old age, I'm the one, and the Connecticut — cherished, protected, valued as the irreplaceable treasure it is — is on its way toward a well-deserved youth
when it will flourish as the centerpiece of the first region in
America that puts aside greed as the only ethic and ugliness
as the only aesthetic and recovers this beautiful wonder
world that on first try we spoiled.

Or so I hope. Me, I'm headed the opposite way, but that's
all right — as long as the river flows in that direction for
me, and for a few hours now and then I can float along with
its current and gain vicariously my own small measure of
renewal and hope.

October now, and the bass have long since gone to their
deep-water haunts, but then a day of warm and radiant sunshine makes me take the canoe down from the loft of our
barn, where I've already stored it for the winter. A quick
gathering of rods and tackle, a note for my wife, a drive
down the mountain, and out onto the Connecticut I go.

The river is full of leaves, leaves of every size, shape, and
color, from vivid gold to impeccable green, the preponder-
ance being double-pronged pine needles of burnt yellow
pointing like delicate arrowheads downstream. It's no trick
at all to align the canoe so it drifts parallel to this autumnal
procession. My fly sinks between leaves and shore, hangs
there in the thick sunlight like a jewel set in honey. Seconds
go by, I'm just about to twitch it, when a bass separates itself
from its own exaggerated shadow there by the rocks, lured
by the same sun that's lured me. The moment I see him I

realize his attention is focused on something in the water, and the moment I realize that something is the streamer the streamer is disappearing, and the moment I realize disappearance and bass have some essential interconnection there's a jolt as the fish takes hold, and then he's soaring through the air, higher and higher, up over the rocks, up over the banks, up over the spruce trees into the realm of sky-colored remembrance where, if I'm lucky, if I ease off on the pressure and don't pull too hard, he will never, not in a dozen years, not in a hundred, come down.

August 13

Summer ritual is a sacred thing, but nowhere more than on Cape Cod. We've come down this weekend for a badly needed fix of sand, sea, and sky — for these, and to touch bases with the much-loved traditions of summers past.

Arriving at our friends' house shortly after breakfast, we're immediately taken on the rounds. The garden to see the state of the corn, the deck to see how far David's extension has proceeded, the aquarium to see John-David's periwinkles, the kitchen to see the crabs Katherine has shredded for a lunchtime salad. Finally, after we've seen everything else — after the summer's adventures and misadventures have been quickly chronicled, to be elaborated upon and embroidered that night over dinner — we're taken down the oak-covered bank to see the biggest surprise of all. There, nestled comfortably against the weathered dock, a spanking new eighteen-foot Boston Whaler, heavy spinning rods mounted in the gimbals, silver gaff propped behind the steering wheel, green landing net — sized for whales — fluttering limply over the flagpole in the stern.

John-David, at twelve, has the fishing bug and has it badly. It's good to watch him caught up in it — to see myself in the obsessive way he ties and reties knots, his agonized indecision when it comes to lures, the importance attached to wearing just the right kind of battered straw hat . . . better still to watch his dad bring to this the same kind of patience, bewilderment, and grace my father brought to my own equally dogmatic boyhood fussings.

Sandwiches packed? Plenty of juice? How's the gas? The nonfishers come down to see us off, and for a time there's enough excitement and merriment on the side of the dock to see off the *QEII*. Our boasts become mixed with their best wishes, then the water is separating us, until finally all that can be heard is the hoarse bark of the family Chesapeake, in despair at being left behind, and we're on our way down the pond, ducking our heads as we go under the low causeway that crosses the inlet, then standing straight again, grabbing onto the side rails as the boat comes bow-first into the choppy waters of Vineyard Sound.

David sets a course alongshore in the smoothest water, but even so, we're in for a good bumping. Out to port is the Vineyard; "like a low smoky cloud," I once described it in a story, but today the haze is blown away and the cloud has become a felt-tipped line of green and tan.

It's nice to play guest for a change, have someone else be in charge of figuring out where the fish might be. Father and son confer over the sound of the motor, decide we're best off in the lee of Nobska Lighthouse toward Wood's Hole. Fine with me — some of the best moments of my life have been spent in and around that busy harbor, and bouncing off it in a small boat is the one perspective I haven't tried.

Any doubt we have is overcome by the sight of gulls and terns sniping at the water off a buoy-marked reef straight out from the Steamship Authority pier. Baitfish are everywhere — they shoot across the surface like silver darts. David brings the boat up to where they're thickest while John-David and I ready our rods. Three or four other boats have raced out from Eel Pond, attracted by these same birds. We form a ring around them — these fish are surrounded! — and in between casts glance around to see who wins this instant, undeclared derby and catches the first blue.

Woods Hole is an interesting enough place to fish, what with ferries coming in from the islands, a fleet of yachts running past, the tide that springs furiously between Buzzards Bay and the Sound. These are all fairly routine, of course, but then the *Oceanus* comes out, the Oceanographic Institute's famous research vessel bound who knows where, and cradled in the stern, its name clearly legible, is the *Alvin*, the homely submersible that found the *Titanic*. To a rube used to fishing the quiet places of the country, it's all quite a show, and it takes the hard, vicious strike of a bluefish to recall me to the water.

It's a modest blue, two pounds at the most, and nowhere near as big as the twelve-pounder John-David landed earlier in the summer. But still, it's the only fish taken, and upholds the undeserved reputation I have after writing a fishing book or two. We bounce around some more, try spots closer in toward shore, then, with not much cooking, turn around and race back along the beaches toward home.

Later that evening, reading the paper, we learn we're not the only ones to have gone blue fishing on this perfect August day. Down in Maine, the President has been taking out his powerboat in the hopes of getting some fish. The papers have been keeping score; to date, it's seven vacation days for the President with not a single blue landed or hooked.

The President, questioned about this, has an excuse. Is it a knowledgeable explanation of bluefish migratory patterns, a normal fisherman-type rationale, a shrug at the wrong kind of weather or the fickleness of fate? No, not at all. The President, having used "environment" as a buzzword during his election campaign, having tried his hardest to open the Gulf of Maine to offshore drilling, having done everything he can to sabotage international efforts to come to grips with global warming and the devastation of acid rain, having placed people in charge of this country's wilderness who are dedicated exploiters of that wilderness, having, in short, done everything he possibly can do to destroy the natural world in which the bluefish swims, now voices his displeasure at not catching one by blaming the press boats, which, in his words, "Come too close and scare the fish away."

I feel bad for the President. But not to despair; two days later, on the last afternoon before he's due to return to Washington, he manages to catch a solitary bluefish, which is then held up for the despised press to record on film.

It's an angry-looking fish, like all blues, but seems angrier than most I've seen, even in death; it's sharp bullet mouth is drawn back in a contemptuous sneer toward the aging man that lifts it. Perhaps it's my imagination at work here, but I see that bluefish as heroic — as the agent of the natural world the President and his cronies have declared war on in their greedy crusade . . . a fish sent on a suicide mission to penetrate the circle of Secret Service boats and press launches and the barges of the President's flunkies — to penetrate and deliver to the President as it's removed from the hook a sharp nip on the hand. Not a fatal nip — nature is too generous for that and there are laws forbidding anything greater — but just enough to make him pay attention.

Did it succeed? Well, in the newspaper pictures the President looks just as inattentive as ever. But it's a sign of rebellious stirrings, a straw in the wind, and makes me feel better about the future of this country than I have in a long time.

Glory and honor onto you, O noble blue!

Two Places Well:
Notes from the West Highlands

That Scotland has a secret becomes apparent to any traveler driving north from the Great Glen. The way the landscape is held back under the serene mist, the hills with their convoluted folds and cloud-draped summits, the open heather that both exaggerates distance and diminishes it, the one-track roads that seem to swallow up cars, literally erase them, the abandoned crofts with their missing roofs, the odd sensation, all but unique on this overcrowded planet, of being in a place that for two centuries has been losing population. It's a secret kept by offering so many possibilities it's impossible to determine which holds the key. Not for nothing is Loch Ness situated in the Highlands — this is a place where surfaces, alluring as they are, only make you want to plunge deeper to grasp what's beneath.

It's a familiar note to any New Englander, at least one who can remember the old days before the interstates when the abandoned hill farms and overgrown meadows suggested both a great loneliness and a great calm. Montana would be the closest you could come to it in the States today — that high, sky-drenched plateau fit for ruminants and ruminators, philosophers and sheep.

Introspection, of course, can be a troublesome thing. There are those who hate the Highlands, hate the way the hills seem to offer something they immediately — the weather being what it is — take back. There are still others who are sensitive to these moods, but vaguely afraid of them; the endless gift shops with their tartan plaids and heather sprigs and shortbread tins seemed designed just for them. "My God, Willa, will you look at that sunset!" "Yes, Donald, but shall we bring Alice home the porridge or this box of Edinburgh Rock?"

But not to laugh at these tourists — the emigrant Scots among them are homesick, the Sassenachs merely confused. Even someone sensitive to landscape has a tough enough time of it here. The weather and terrain change so fast it's possible to read into Highland scenery any conclusion you want. Life is this, life is that, and so many in-betweens it makes you dizzy.

So much weight for a land so small! But it's exactly the West Highlands' charm, this association of opposites, the intimate grandeur, this cozy expanse. Take the road south along the coast from Ullapool and you'll see what I mean. There to the right is the ocean, wild and cold-looking; there to the left, mountains even wilder and colder; in between along the roadside, a jungle of lush rhododendron that seems lifted from Henri Rousseau. Better yet, screw up your courage and drive the Pass of the Cattle inland from Applecross farther down the coast, glancing up at the scenery in those brief intervals when the road straightens from its switch-backing descent. Hills on one side, sea on the other, lochs in between, the three elements repeated in endless superimpositions of color, line, and plane.

And if the land is dense in scenery, it is even denser in history, so that the past in Scotland is as exposed and palpable as the heather and rocks. These human associations are always poignant, often tragic — too many seem to memorialize farewells. The plaques in village kirks commemorating soldiers dead in foreign wars; those shortbread tins showing Bonnie Prince Charlie bidding a respectful adieu to Flora Macdonald; the marker indicating the spot Mary Stuart left Scotland on her way to being axed; the emigrant ports with their sad reminders of the Clearances, when crofters were forced off the land by their lairds to make way for sheep. . . . Travel through these glens and you're never far from a good-bye that was forced.

Clearance, war, emigration, neglect — such has been the Highland lot since the Jacobite insurrection and the bitter Culloden defeat. Bad enough in the past, there is a new round of clearances under way today, the so-called "Second Clearance" as the current lairds (who when it comes to insensitive greed could teach American developers a thing or two) clear the sheep off the hills in order to plant more profitable spruce.

The one who would know about this cycle best — the man around whose bronze shoulders the secret of Scotland seems to drape — stands with an old model Lee-Enfield rifle on the outskirts of Glenelg, his kilted legs planted firmly on the pebbly marge of the shingle, his mustached face, tarnished by salt water, looking out toward the mountains of

Skye across the narrow, whitecapped Sound of Sleat. He
stands there for a reason — to commemorate the final chapter in the Scots diaspora, the half-forced, half-voluntary
emigration to the trenches of Flanders and France in what is
still known in the Highlands as the Great War.

Never was a statue better placed. Remote, solitary, its
loneliness set against scenery that is almost unbearable in its
perfection, it evokes as no words can the tragic loss of those
years 1914–18, when the Highlander, the man who had
withstood all history could throw at him, was all but
destroyed as a separate proud being by the wicked expe-
diency of Maxim machine guns and coiled concertina wire.

Glenelg is neither an easy place to find nor to drive to —
it's as if to approach the statue you must first traverse
enough Highland landscape that it settles deep into your
understanding. The stoic and bitter — these are plain
enough in the erect way the soldier stands there, the simple
inscription on the plate. But there's beauty in it, too, the
other half of the secret, and if you stand there long enough,
waiting for that slow summer sun to get below the Cullins,
you'll see the secret toward which everything in the Highlands seems trending — the dark bittersweet shadow of a
place history has blessed by leaving behind.

I visited Glenelg last year, spent my hour at the base of
the statue, then wandered down to the water to see if I
couldn't skim a rock all the way to Skye. Celeste was with
me — I had spent the first years of our marriage attempting
to describe to her the beauty of the Highlands, deciding in
the end the only way to do it was to let her see for herself.
And though we spent a lot of time at it, we weren't there
simply to define what it was we found so alluring in the

landscape, but to actually immerse ourselves *in* some. For the first half of our trip this meant climbing, or as they more correctly call it in this part of the world, "hill walking." We'd gone up Lochnagar from the Spittal of Glen Muick on a brutally hot afternoon, and had been rewarded at the top by a view of the famous Black Spout gully and the silvery lochan nestled below its sheer walls. We hill walked around Glencoe, too, getting lost just long enough in a snow squall to be able to laugh about it later as we nursed some Courage in a Fort William pub.

Now here we were in the West Highlands turning our attention from hills to trout lochs — the lochs that had, on my earlier visit, both enchanted me and, having neither the time nor means to fish them, tormented me as well. We made our base at the fishing lodge in Shieldaig near Gairloch; situated right on the ocean, they have the rights to the fishing on a dozen hill lochs scattered back a good ten miles inland.

It's beyond expectation that a place that suits me so well in every other respect should have trout in it as well. The Highlands are full of fish, browns brightly colored and wild. Such is their abundance that bags over a hundred are not uncommon, at least up in Sutherland, and nobody thinks the worst of you for keeping all you want. Add to this the salmon rivers, sea trout streams, and hill burns, not only on the mainland but in the Hebrides, the Shetlands, and Orkney, and you have a place where the fly-fishing opportunities are endless. Read the Brit fishing magazines (which are wonderfully chatty and specific compared to ours), and you can get a quick overview of all this and the names of generous fishermen who are more than willing to help you with advice.

This was my first experience of British fishing, and I was more than a little intimidated by what I'd read of its tradition. Wasn't this where you were guilty of terribly bad manners if you used anything besides the fly the trout were actually taking? Where people called river "keepers" lurked behind the boxberry, the better to catch you out? Where — for all I knew — you were expected to bow to other fishermen you passed, or maybe not bow at all, but put your nose up in the air and snort, "Good nymphing, what?," failing which you were taken off the water and expelled to the rude place whence you came?

Maybe this is so in England, but up north in the hills there's a more relaxed ethic at work. In the Shieldaig lodge's lobby is a list of all the lochs, and you pick out one that's free, write your name down beside it, help yourself to the keys to its rowboat, and you're in business. Arriving late in the afternoon as we did, we were too late to bid, but this was no problem either; Colin, the lodge's owner, explained we were free to fish any loch we wanted, as long as we cast from shore and didn't use a boat.

Fine. I put our rods together, Celeste grabbed her pack, and into it we stuffed gammon sandwiches put up by the hotel's chef, some scones, and — the pack having just enough room — a bottle of white Hungarian wine.

We decided to try the closest loch first. It's an uphill two-mile walk, and we took our time with it since the sun was as bright and hot as it had been our entire trip (at dinner that night the other fishermen complained bitterly about the weather being *too good*). Spring lambing was over, and the lambs were everywhere — they were just old enough to leave their mothers' sides, but would stumble back in confusion the moment they saw us. Somewhere along the way

I glanced down at my watch; it was four on the button, and to prove it the watch cuckooed.

It wasn't the watch, of course, but a real cuckoo, whose call, though we'd heard it often on our walks, we still couldn't convince ourselves was real.

"It's over there," I said, pointing.

Celeste listened with her head tilted. "No, further away. Over . . . there."

"It could make you cuckoo playing this game."

"Cu-kooo. Cu-kooo." This from the bird.

The loch, once we got there, was larger than I'd pictured, the size of water that would have been crowded with cottages back home. Here, there was no sign of any human presence, nothing except a rowboat on the far shore with a solitary fly-fisherman whose rod, enlarged by the sun, lay tilted like a stirrer in a punch bowl of gold.

I was worried about the fishing-from-shore business, but there were no trees here, nothing but heather, and when it came to backcasting room the sky was literally the limit. On my second cast, a brown came up from the peat-colored depths, curled its body around the fly, then — just when I thought he had missed it — came tight against the line. He wasn't big, perhaps half a pound at the most, but even from the distance I could see the butter-crimson blend of his color, and he fought in an exuberant, bulldogging manner reminiscent of smallmouth bass.

I caught three more after that; initiated, I rock-hopped along shore to where Celeste was trying her best to keep her line free of the heather. It was hot, the fish were feeding just out of her range, my advice wasn't particularly tactful, and between one thing and the other it was suggested I walk a little way off so she could fish alone. Meaning to save her the effort, I swung the rucksack up on my back; a little farther along, I bent over to tie my boots and out the opened flap of the pack directly into the water dropped Celeste's favorite Nikon camera.

I fished it out again, but the lens and viewfinder were soaked. Celeste, hearing the splash, came over to see what I had caught.

"We can let it dry," I said lamely.

"It's ruined. Absolutely ruined."

"I guess you should have tied the flap up."

Counterattacking is always a big mistake. Celeste dropped her rod into the heather, grabbed the camera, and stalked off in the direction of the lodge. Under any other circumstances I would have hurried after her, but behind me the trout were beginning to rise, and not just occasionally but *everywhere*. I was mad at her for leaving, madder yet at my clumsiness, but grateful, too — at least she had left the rod! Thus equipped, I could switch from a sinking line to a floating one without changing spools.

Despite the rises, the trout preferred taking the fly just as it became waterlogged and sank. Once I figured this out, I caught fish regularly. The sun setting so late in Scotland, it was tempting to stay long enough to bring the total up to two dozen or three, but I was worried about Celeste, and after my thirteenth I put the rods up and walked back to the lodge.

Things smoothed out over a dinner of trout and the bottle of wine. We talked to Colin and decided to reserve the farthest loch for the next day. It was a two-hour hike, but supposedly the fishing was worth it.

We got an early start in the morning, or at least tried to — when we went to fetch the key to the boat on our loch, it couldn't be found. We asked Colin, who asked the night clerk, who asked the chambermaid, but without success — the key had gone missing. I suspect we upstart Yanks were being none too subtly bumped off a loch, but there didn't seem to be much we could do about it. The only loch still available was the one we had already fished, but maybe, we told ourselves, the sacrifice of the camera would have propitiated the gods there in our favor.

And apparently it had — our day there was perfect, from the moment I pushed Celeste out from the beach in the skiff and jumped in after her, to the moment eight hours later when we slid the boat back into the sandy impression left by the keel. We caught trout, a large number, and they seemed the vibrant, living underline to the generous blue sky and the easy June breeze and a waterscape set like liquid heather against the hills.

The skiff was a heavy one of traditional design, with thick green planking, iron oarlocks, and a healthy amount of daylight showing between her ribs. She was heavy to push out, a lot heavier to row — a good heavy, I decided. It slowed down the drifting and got me thinking.

"You know," I said, digging in the oars. "This American fascination . . . *puff* . . . for lightweight equipment . . . *puff* . . . has gotten out of hand. There's a lot to be said for old-fashioned solid construction . . . *puff* . . . as exemplified . . . *puff* . . . by this skiff."

"Hmmmmn?" Celeste responded, looking up from her fly. "Could you please row a little faster, dear? I think Scots trout prefer more speed."

"Certainly. But what I meant to say . . . *puff puff puff* . . . is that less is not necessarily . . . Just let me rest here for a moment . . . *phew* . . . more."

With a boat like that, anchoring was almost redundant. I gave a final desperate yank on the oars and we glided to a stop in a cove where the shoreline dropped sheer in a mica-flecked cliff. Celeste immediately caught a nice one-pound brown that ran toward the rock as if to climb it. My arms ached so much from rowing it was all I could do to cast at all, but then I caught one, too, and immediately decided — now that the ice was broken — to tie on something I'd been wanting to try for a long time.

It was a cast — a leader — of three wet flies. Once upon a time it was a common way to fish in the States, and there were passionate arguments concerning which order the flies should be arranged in and why. There's probably not a Yank under the age of eighty-five who remembers this method, but in Scotland it's still a common way to fish, and at a tackle store in Edinburgh I'd bought several of the dropper-festooned leaders and a handful of appropriate flies.

I rummaged through them now, picked out three I thought offered the fish the most variety, thereby emphasizing their smorgasbord attraction. They weren't easy to cast (not just for the wind do the Scots use those heavy rods), but I finally managed to get the slow, deliberate roll of it and work out line.

The trout, as if to encourage me in my first clumsy attempt to speak Scots, immediately responded. A fat speedy fish came a fantastic distance to take the red fly at the end, and before I could bring him in, another had taken a swipe at the brown fly in the middle. Whether it was the processional quality of the flies, their resemblance to a school of baitfish, or simply the greater odds of the multiple offerings, the trout kept slashing at my rig with happy abandon. It was fascinating to see which fly caught the most; as it turned out, it was the red one at the end. The fish, having seen the first two sail by, couldn't resist a shot at the shimmery third.

At lunchtime, we rowed across the loch to where a burn spilled across a broken weir, and ate our sandwiches looking toward the grayish blue hills in the east. They were twenty miles away, but such was the transparency of the air, the treeless intervention, they seemed much closer. They had an airy, detached look, as if they were hovering above the moors; the sight, combined with the spray of the burn, took the place of the vanished breeze to cool us off.

A sea gull drifted in from the ocean to look us over. Watching it, we saw a raven circling even slower, in a higher orbit, and watching the raven, trying to focus against the sun, we saw a still-higher shape, an eagle, all but motionless it was so high, as if loch, hills, and birds all circled around the brown fixed center of its wings.

The afternoon was largely an expansion of the morning, with more trout, more sun, and the funny footnote of lambs coming down to the edge of the loch to look us over. On our way back to the lodge, on a whim, we detoured off on a trail to what are called the Fairy Lochs — three interconnected lochs set high on a miniature plateau.

"Hear it?" Celeste said, as we paused to catch our breaths.

I glanced at my watch. "Four o'clock. Right on schedule."

There were no jokes about cuckoos this time — we kept on climbing. The lochs, once we got there, reminded me of the remote ponds we have back in New England, minus the trees. Celeste stretched out on the heather to nap while I made my way around the perimeter of each one, trying a few casts, exploring, not really caring if I caught fish or not.

As I completed my circuit and made my way back I

noticed something scattered in the heather and by it partially obscured: bright shiny pieces of metal. Some of them were small and curled like shavings, but some were ruler-sized, and one piece was as long as my arm and violently bent.

What I was looking at was the scattered wreckage of an army transport that had crashed on its way back to the States in June of 1945. We got the story later from Colin. The plane had been full of returning GI's, and it had hit against the plateau's summit during a storm, killing all thirty aboard. A band of local farmers and ghillies had climbed through the snow and gotten to the bodies first; a shred of brown fabric had been their first clue, and then there was more of it, until it was as if they were following a deliberately laid trail of torn uniforms.

It's a sad and eerie sight, that unstainable silver metal. It's American, but the touch is unmistakably Highland — the bitter under the sweet, the farewell that is tragic, the ghosts amid lochans meant for fairies, fishermen, and trout.

I can catch wild one-pound trout for a long time without getting bored, but after another day on the lochs we decided to take a break from the fishing in order to make a literary pilgrimage to a place I had wanted to see since I was a boy: Camusfearna, the remote coastal home made famous by Gavin Maxwell in his 1960 best-seller about otters, *Ring of Bright Water.*

Maxwell is all but forgotten in America, I suppose, but he's still in print in Britain, and thirty years ago his books were as popular as Joy Adamson's *Born Free* series about Elsa and her cubs. It was a time of dawning environmental consciousness, an awakening to the fact we were exterminating so many species, and at some level people probably wanted to be told the animals forgave us for this — that lions would lie beside our cots at night in perfect contentment; that otters, for all our sins, bore us no grudge.

Maxwell was a lyrical writer, and reading his books as a child I was even more enchanted with his descriptions of the lonely Highland setting of Camusfearna than I was by the otters. An old sea-weathered house set on a beach where no one could bother you, with nothing to do all day but the chores of running the place, a spot of beachcombing, then long, slow evenings filled with books? It was the kind of place Holden Caulfield was looking for; it was the kind of place *I* was looking for, even at twelve, and the magic of his evocation settled so deeply it became at least partially responsible for who I turned out to be.

Camusfearna wasn't its real name, but a protective alias. "This is from no desire to create mystery," Maxwell wrote, "but because identification in print would seem in some sense a sacrifice, a betrayal of its remoteness and isolation, as if by doing so I were to bring nearer its enemies of industry and urban life. Camusfearna, I have called it, the Bay of the Alders."

Maxwell could have had no way of knowing, writing those lines, how immensely popular his book was to become — and how many thousands of readers would take it into their heads not only to discover where Camusfearna was located, but to visit it in person. He was dogged by sightseers for the next eight years; there is no law of trespass in Scotland, and anyone who happened along had to be put up with. By the time he came to write the third book in the Camusfearna trilogy, *Raven Seek Thy Brother*, the disguise hardly seemed worth the effort. "It will be obvious to any interested reader that Camusfearna is Sandaig, by

Sandaig Lighthouse, on the mainland of Scotland some five miles south of Glenelg village."

And five miles south of Glenelg village is where we were driving, visors down to keep the sun from our eyes, Maxwell's book open on the dashboard like a compass pointing the way. There over the cliff on our right was a sand-fringed promontory jutting out into the Sound of Sleat — Sandaig Lighthouse, we decided — and a little farther up the road stood a simple green cottage that was boarded up and empty.

"This must be the Macleods' house," I said, slowing down to park.

"The who?" Celeste asked.

"The family who lived here when Maxwell did. He was always writing about them. They were his support system. No, more than that. They were his link to the human race."

The next part should have been easy, but wasn't. We knew where Sandaig Lighthouse was — we had the cottage at our backs — but that still left a large space in between with nothing to point the way. Since Maxwell's day the bare, bracken-covered cliff has grown over with Sitka and larch, and the forest is high and thick enough to obscure the views in every direction.

There were some overgrown woods roads, nothing more. We took the one that pointed most directly toward the ocean, and almost immediately came upon our next clue: a burn, a narrow, primrose-lined burn that dropped out of sight in the direction of the coast.

Anyone who's read Maxwell remembers All Na Fearna, the Alder burn — how important it was to the life of Camusfearna, both as a source of drinking water and as a playground for the otters Edal and Mij. In *Ring of Bright*

Water he describes balancing his way down it when he first came here to live.

"Presently the burn became narrower, and afforded no footholds on its steep banks, then it tilted sharply seaward between rock walls, and below me I could hear the roar of a high waterfall. I climbed out from the ravine, and found myself on a bluff of heather and red bracken looking down upon the sea and upon Camusfearna."

This was the fastest way down then, but the waterfall part made me hesitate — despite the drought, the burn was high with snowmelt from nearby Ben Sgriol — and so we decided to try and find an alternate route. I won't list all our false starts and disappointed backtrackings, other than to say that finally, just when we were about to give up, we found something all but miraculous scratched there in the dirt beneath our feet: an arrow pointing toward a vague break in the Sitka near the cliff's edge.

"Shall we try it?" Celeste asked.

"Someone must have drawn it for their friends to follow," I said. Then, shrugging: "Sure, why not?"

The gap in the Sitka grew larger, we came upon some poles carrying a single strand of wire, the path widened and dipped, and then suddenly there we were on the edge of the cliff staring down at the scene that had greeted Maxwell the morning of his first glorious descent.

> The landscape and seascape that lay spread below me was of such beauty that I had no room for it all at once; my eyes flickered from the house to the islands, from the white sands to the flat green pasture round the croft, from the wheeling gulls to the pale satin sea and on to the snow-tipped Cuillins

of Skye in the distance. . . . Immediately below me the steep
hillside of heather and ochre mounting grasses fell to a broad
green field, almost an island, for the burn flanked it at the
right and then curved round seaward in a glittering horse-
shoe. The sea took up where the burn left off, and its fore-
shore formed the whole frontage of the field, running up
nearest to me in a bay of rocks and sand. At the edge of this
bay, a stone's throw from the sea on one side and the burn
on the other, the house of Camusfearna stood unfenced in
green grass.

Staring down at this my mind raced with the frantic
regauging that comes when you finally see a place in person
you've fallen in love with through books. There below us
was a grassy meadow waving in the breeze, a corner of sea
that was almost tropic in its turquoise, the bright, pebbly
curve of burn that suggested Maxwell's title — all these,
and not just flat as they come off the page, but round and
splashy and colored, with the rolling bass note of incoming
breakers and the sandier hiss of their retreat. Beyond the
burn were the ridges of the miniature islands, and beyond
these, repeating their anticlines with more emphasis, the
first blue mountains of Skye.

It was just as Maxwell described — with the exception of
the house. On January 20, 1968, it burned to the ground,
and the ruins were later bulldozed over, so that except for a
small memorial marking the spot where Maxwell's ashes
were spread when he died the next year, there is nothing left
of it whatsoever, not even its foundation.

We climbed the rest of the way down to the grass,
instinctively lowering our voices, not so much out of respect,
but at the pure shattering beauty of the spot. Meadow,

beach, ocean, burn. Here in front of us were perfect speci-
mens of each, as if nature had decided to show exactly what
she could do with each form in the briefest possible compass,
and then display them beneath a sun and sky that were perfect, too.

Knowing nothing of Maxwell, coming here quite by
chance, you would still sense something bittersweet in this
scene, breathtaking as it is. Simply put, it's hard to look at
all this and not want in some way to *want* it. No, not want
it. Want never to *leave* — to have the ability to open one's
eyes each morning on exactly this landscape, and not just
for an afternoon, not just for a summer or even a lifetime,
but *forever.*

It's too much to want of a place — if nothing else, Maxwell's life here was evidence of this. His books, for all their
delight, read like an endless shopping list of misfortune.
Lawsuits, accidents, sinkings, divorce, illness, the killing of
Mijibal, his first otter, more accidents, more illness, more
sinkings — not without reason, Maxwell ended up believing
he was cursed.

These calamities have an unintended effect, as depressing
as they are — they reinforce his picture of Camusfearna as
sanctuary, a preserve surrounded by danger on every side.
Even at twelve I responded to this, and it's clear, the modern
world being what it is, this note gave the book much of its
appeal. "Whatever you're going to do in the future," a
reader wrote him, "please never say that the Camusfearna
of *Ring of Bright Water* never was. Say that it's gone, if
you like, but not that you lied. I couldn't take that, because
it was the only evidence I had that Paradise existed
somewhere."

Well, Maxwell did in effect say all this — that in the end

life was too much for him, and even the love of otters couldn't pull him through. There can't be too many examples of a writer creating a dream in so many hearts and then taking such pains to shatter it, but perhaps Maxwell can only be blamed for not shattering it correctly — for not taking pains to explain that Camusfearna, seen on an afternoon like this one, was so perfect it made you all but sob at the limitations of mortality.

We didn't sob. We stared at all this, felt these things, then went down to the beach to take a closer look. It's to the left of where the house was located, curving inward for a longer distance than I had pictured. The breeze was just strong enough to add manes to the waves lazing in through the turquoise — again, the effect was tropical. Celeste took off her shoes and waded across the burn's mouth to the first miniature island; an old boat was cast up and neglected there on the rocks, undoubtedly one of Maxwell's shipwrecked fleet, though her name had long since been weathered off the stern.

We spent an hour or more beyond the burn, bending down to examine the wild roses, picking up pieces of shell and brightly colored pebbles, turning over the wooden fish boxes that had drifted ashore (in Maxwell's time, they had been the chief source of Camusfearna's furniture). When the tide turned, we retraced our footsteps back across the burn. There was an English couple sitting in the grass beside Maxwell's stone; the man was reading a paperback edition of *Ring of Bright Water*. We talked for a while. No, he had never heard of the book before, not until coming up to Scotland. Yes, it was good to look up from the page and see illustrations, as it were, of what he was reading.

To the rear of the meadow, tucked in a fold of the cliff, is the waterfall and the basin that served as Camusfearna's swimming hole, not just for its human inhabitants, but the otters as well. It's high and serene and rocky, so that resting on the ferns by its edge, smelling the wild garlic, it's hard to remember you're not deep in mountains but only a Frisbee toss from the sea.

We plunked our toes into the frigid water, then pulled them quickly back out. Sitting there we could summon up a happier Camusfearna, the haven where Maxwell brought his otters to let them roam free.

"She rejoiced in the waves," he says, writing of Edal, his second otter.

> She would hurl herself straight as an arrow right into the great roaring gray wall of an oncoming breaker and go clean through it as if it had neither weight nor momentum; she would swim far out to sea through wave after wave until the black dot of her head was lost among the distant white manes, and more than once I thought that some wild urge to seek new land had dizzied her and that she would go on swimming west in the Sea of the Hebrides and that I should not see her again.

Eventually, with all the disasters that befell Camusfearna and its owner, Edal had to be kept locked up in the house. In *Raven Seek Thy Brother*, Maxwell describes the gradual reestablishment of their trust, and how they were at last able to resume much of their old life together . . . a life that was destroyed when, after so many new beginnings, the house burned and Edal with it. She is buried beside the burn underneath a rowan tree; on the flat top of the rocky monument is cut the epitaph *Edal, the otter of Ring of Bright Water, 1958–68. Whatever joy she gave to you, give back to nature.*

On the weathered metal beside these words we found earlier visitors had left their small tributes — a shell, a twist of flower, a small blue feather shed by a bird. Celeste walked over to the beach, found a stone that was white and perfectly oval, then — tapping the other gifts gently aside to make room — added its brightness to Edal's collection.

Maxwell wasn't the only one we were reading on the hills. There was John Inglis Hall's *Fishing a Highland Stream*, about the Truim, Robin Ade's *Fisher in the Hills*, about the burns and lochans of Galloway, and, with special enjoyment, the novels of a writer who was famous in Scotland yet all but unknown in the states, Neil Gunn. Read his *Blood Hunt* and you'll see what a talented novelist could do with this landscape — a landscape where people have enough space between them that they stand out as men and women should stand out, craggy and individual and proud.

Between reading these, driving past salmon rivers and sea trout streams we wouldn't have time for, hearing stories in the pubs about the fabulous lochs in Sutherland and the Orkneys, we were storing up resolutions about where we would fish on our next trip. As for *this* one, there were only two days left now before our plane left Prestwick — just enough time to take care of what for me was some very important unfinished business.

It didn't concern trout this time, but mountains — one mountain in particular. On my first trip to Scotland, nine years before, traveling mainly by bus and foot, I had

splurged one morning, rented a car in Inverness, and driven
northwestward toward the coast. I ended up in Ullapool
around three — it was November and the shops and hotels
were shuttered closed. I found a chips shop down by the
harbor, and nursed a cup of coffee while I watched a rusty
trawler unload its catch. Finishing, I decided to drive a bit
farther on, look the scenery over, then turn back toward
Inverness.

I hadn't gone far when I saw a man beside the road with
his thumb stuck out. Ordinarily, I'm wary of picking up
hitchhikers, but in this kind of emptiness it seemed a moral
imperative to stop.

"How far you going?" I asked, rolling down the window.

The man was already opening the passenger door, sliding
himself in. "Not far," he said, or something like it. "Oh,
just up the road a way."

He was an angular, ruddy-faced man in his twenties,
dressed in a brown duffle coat patched with tape. His "just
up the road" turned out to be twenty miles along a one-track
road through the grandest hill scenery I had ever seen in my
life — grandest, and with the sun going down, the road getting twistier, loneliest. It turned out he was a mason working in a village called Achiltibuie on the coast facing the
Summer Islands, a small chain of the Inner Hebrides. In the
usual Highland pattern, the government was moving everyone off these islands into the equivalent of council houses
on the mainland — houses he was involved with building.

"What does Achiltibuie mean?" I asked him.

"The place where the fair-haired boy lives," he answered.

I nodded. "Does he live there still?"

It was a throwaway line, but its effect was as if I had just stuck my finger in his ribs and started twisting. He laughed so hard he toppled sideways against the car door. For minutes he laughed; he would recover himself, take a deep breath, remember what I'd said, then start off laughing again, his whole body wracked with spasms. For all I know they speak of my reply in Achiltibuie to this day as the wittiest thing ever said there; "Aye, he was a grand comedian, that Yank," someone will say, shaking his head in nostalgic admiration.

Despite the communication gap of his Gallic swallowings and my New Yorkese, we were old buddies by the time we made it to the village. I stayed long enough for a mug of whiskey, then started back along the road far faster than I'd driven up it, trying to reach pavement before the light disappeared.

"And what happened then?" Celeste asked. We were driving the opposite way along this same road now, on a bright sunny day nine years later.

"My left front tire went flat."

"Right here?"

"Up ahead somewhere, I think. It was almost dark. Luckily, there was a spare in the boot. I changed it, then just before I got back in the car saw something that had been there right behind me all along."

"A sheep?"

I shook my head. "A mountain."

And not just any mountain, but one so unusual and compelling I fell in love with it at first sight. There rising above me in the darkness from a slope of scree, its sides barely outlined as a richer shade of black against the dark northern sky, was a crenellated ridge of abrupt towers and weird spires that in variety and steepness would have made a fit play-

ground for trolls. It was like looking up at the walls of a
fantasy castle in Spain, a bit of Yosemite transported to the
Highlands, a . . . Well, all my comparisons were feeble. It
wasn't the highest mountain I'd ever seen, not even the
most spectacular, but between its isolation there by the sea
and the abruptness of those towers, it was impossible to look
at it and not want to stand on top.

It wasn't until the following morning back in Inverness
that I discovered this beautiful and suggestive peak had a
beautiful and suggestive name: Stac Polly. The book I found
it in was called *The Scottish Peaks* by one W. A. Poucher,
who describes it lovingly thus:

> This peak with its bristling summit ridge of sandstone pin-
> nacles is the favorite of all mountaineers visiting Coigach.
> Bold and steep buttresses rise at each end of the mountain;
> the weird formations of sandstone are a great attraction and
> those crowning the terminal points of some of the very nar-
> row spurs can only be reached by a sensational scramble. The
> whole of Stac Polly is the delight of the photographer, and is
> the most rewarding and sensational subject in all Scotland.

I brought the book back to the States with me, glanced at
Stac Polly's picture surprisingly often in the intervening
years, daydreamed about going back one day and climbing
it. Gradually, it became one of those lesser ambitions even
a happy life becomes littered with, and yet fate took a lucky
turn with this one, and here I was nine years later parking
my car in the turnoff at its base and tying on my hiking
boots and starting toward its ridge with my wife.

Again, we were blessed with the sunshine that had
drenched us every minute of the trip. Between the darkness
of the night I'd first seen it and the natural exaggeration of

memory, I was prepared to be disappointed by Stac Polly's size, but if anything the sun only emphasized it, throwing the towers and spires into even bolder relief. I understood now the appropriateness of the name. Weathered indents made the towers look stacked rather than carved, and homely as the mountain was, there was a wild, merry impudence in the way it rose there from the scree — a perfect Polly through and through.

Our legs were in that happy condition that comes after a week's strenuous climbing, when up hardly seems up at all, and we made good time along the dry bed of a burn. There were lots of sheep about with their lambs; in a short while we were above them, or at least all but one.

"Hear that bleating?" Celeste asked. "It's a lamb. He's stranded up there on the cliff."

"He'll be all right," I said.

"That must be his mother down below. I think you should climb up and chase him back to her."

I wasn't worried about the lamb; he was perched on a ledge fifty yards above us, as rigid and proud as the hood ornament on a '53 Buick. We were out to climb Stac Polly — why deny that privilege to him? But unluckily for the lamb, I was in a frisky mood, and the idea of chasing him from his smugness was irresistible.

Off I went. Within seconds I was in among the lesser towers and buttresses that make up Stac Polly's flank. It was hard to keep sight of the lamb from in close. Celeste, below me on the bulge of scree, kept up a running play-by-play.

"He's still there. . . . No, he's moving through the heather. He's coming your way. He sees you. . . . He's heading uphill. He's trotting. . . . He's trotting faster."

Each time I drew even with him, he took off again, climbing those rocks as daintily as a mountain goat. I doubled back under him, came at him from the steep slope to his left, hid behind a boulder to let him settle, then traversed to the right to take him unawares.

"Gotcha!" I yelled, all but springing.

There was nothing behind the rock. Above me, a long way above me, the lamb stuck out its tongue.

We played this game for an hour in all. When I finally gave up, I was panting from effort, my knickers were torn from briars, Celeste was doubled over with laughter, and the lamb was back in the exact spot he had started, bleating in happiness as his mother trotted past us to fetch him.

"You did good, honey," Celeste said, patting the spot on the shoulders where my ego resides. "Real good."

Chasing lambs doesn't leave much strength for climbing mountains, but we'd come too far to quit now. The trail leveled off, then swung to the right to get around onto the north face. As we turned the corner a whole new view opened up — the country unrolling into Sutherland — but the footing was becoming dicier as the slope steepened, and we couldn't take our eyes off the ground other than to peek.

Toward the top the trail left off switchbacking and went directly up the rocks. The last ten yards would have been rock climbing in the States, but is called "scrambling" in Scotland — scrambling and kicking and scratching and clawing. Celeste got up first, let out a delighted yell, then reached down to help me up the last bit of rock. In a second I was beside her, and together we were looking out at the world falling away beneath our feet.

There to our left were the lower round pillars of Stac Polly, grooved brown by the weather, aligned so they pointed like a gunsight toward the sea. At our backs was the

twisting line of the road up which we had driven — in one
coil was a loch with a fisherman's rowboat moving at the
apex of a green, outspreading V. Directly in front of us,
seemingly endless, stretched the wild country north of the
mountain — a furrowed, treeless expanse of loch and
lochan, moor and hill, with the sea on one side, mountains
on the other, and in between nothing that hinted at the presence of man. In the stillness of that windless day only one
sound could be heard, and it seemed the very call of that
landscape, impossible to locate, distant, unutterably sweet.

"Hear it?" I said.

Celeste smiled. "Cuckoo, our old friend."

In the afternoon slant of sun, the misty softening pro-
vided by the sea, it was at the same time the wildest landscape I'd ever seen and the gentlest. I thought of Thoreau's
happy phrase: "A breadth of view equivalent to motion" —
just looking at it made you soar.

"What's that one called over there?" Celeste said, pointing to the nearest mountain, the one with snow in its gullies.

I turned through the guidebook. "Cul Mor," I said. Then,
flipping to the glossary: "Great Nook."

There were no foothills to these mountains — they rose
directly from the moorland, so they seemed many times
their actual height. The most impressive was wedge-shaped
Suilven directly opposite us over Loch Sionscaig; as often as
we spun around to point at something new, we kept coming
back to it, and when we finally sat down to eat our sandwiches, it was facing Suilven's direction.

We stayed on top with the light. My legs were tired with
satisfaction at having completed the climb, and it was
matched by the kind of contentment that comes when you
find — from the height of years — that one of your ambi-

tions was worth the dreaming after all. For a long time the view alone was enough to occupy me, but then mountains being the metaphoric prompters they are, I tried focusing on some thoughts that seemed as large and compelling as distant Suilven. Story ideas, a rush of remembrance from that earlier, lonelier visit, resolutions for the future, not just about travels, but ambitions and difficult, all but unobtainable goals. I tried capturing them, but they floated off into the soft air, where, measured against that scenery, they popped apart into the fine, scattered mist of insignificance.

But that was all right. One did stay intact, the one I brought down with me, my one and only Highland souvenir. The things we had seen, our small adventures, the sense we'd had in all our circling of coming closer to the secret of these hills. We weren't there yet, not by a long shot, but the challenge was clear now — to take home from the landscape a new breadth of perspective; to keep it in memory; to someday come back again; to learn this key to wisdom . . . to know two places well.

September 30

My hunch is that we fly-fishers, away from the water, measure rather less gullible than average. Fly-fishing, after all, attracts many of its practitioners from the professions that deal with precise measurement of fact on one hand and intuitive gropings toward truth on the other — actuaries and historians, engineers and poets, draftsmen and bakers, scientists and philosophers. Then, too, it's not in front of the television set swallowing lies that we choose to spend our leisure time. No, on the whole, we're rather less gullible than the norm.

We overcompensate for this skepticism once you get us out on the water. There, when it comes to gullibility, we're the biggest suckers there are. You can test this yourself easily enough. Next time you see another fly-fisherman walking along your favorite stream, stop him thus:

"Good morning." (You say.)

"Hi. How's the fishing?" (He says.)

"Not so hot. But I'll tell you what. There's this blonde sunbathing up there in that meadow, I believe she said her name is Miss June or Miss July, something like that, but anyway she needs someone to help her with her suntan lotion. . . ."

Or, as a variation:

"Not so hot. But I'll tell you what. There's this wildcat oil well up there in the meadow all ready to start pumping, all it needs is someone to invest a little more capital. . . ."

Now an ersatz fly-fisherman will perhaps rise to these baits, but a skeptical fly-fisherman, a *genuine* fly-fisherman, won't bat an eye. This is where the real test comes, variation number three:

"Not so hot. But tell you what. There's a three-pound brown sitting in tight by an alder up there in that first pool. I gave him my best shot, but nothing doing. He's all yours."

And off our skeptical fly-fisherman will run, hurrying past you so fast you can all but feel the slipstream of his credulity.

Fiction writers have a term for this: *the willing suspension of disbelief*. What makes it possible, I suppose, is the mystery of the watery element we probe. Measured in cosmological terms, it wasn't that long ago we were water dwellers ourselves, and our hunch that a huge fish might be lurking just beyond that outcrop of coral was the defensive safety mechanism by which our species thrived. Now, emerged, our other instincts dulled, we still remember this one ancestral lesson: in the water, as in the dark, *anything goes*.

Not all waters are created equal in this respect. I find,

fishing a dark muddy pond, that it's hard to believe there are fish in the murkiness; conversely, fishing the Caribbean, where it's no trick at all to see bottom fifty feet down, I find it just as difficult to believe there are fish in such clarity. Hope requires neither transparency nor opaqueness, but flourishes best in exactly the right blend — the transparency of a trout stream, say, where we can see just far enough into the bright swirls of color to make of them huge fishy forms.

I was given a good refresher lesson in all this yesterday afternoon. I was down on the White River, famous water in New England, but for me — with all the best intentions in the world — a stream with which I've never quite hit it off. The water's always too high when I get there, or too low; there are lots of fishermen about, lots of canoes, and the presence of the interstate, in an already sloppy valley, pretty well spoils most of its charm. Still, there are serious fish in the White, big rainbows I've seen racing away from my boots, and the salmon restoration effort has, if nothing else, drawn to its banks a loyal band of river advocates I admire very much. Between this and the undeniable beauty of the remoter stretches, the White and I have reached a grudging truce over the years: it gives me a trout or two each time I visit; I don't push it and don't bad-mouth it to my friends.

Yesterday I drove up past Stockbridge, where the river narrows to a width you can pretty well cover in one cast. Even so, I had to watch my footing; as relaxed as the river is there, there are surprisingly deep holes. For the first hour I spent most of my time freeing my hook from the salmon parr that throw themselves on even the biggest dry fly with maniacal persistence, as if demonstrating they have the moxie it takes to swim round-trip to Greenland. There was a trout where the flow was smoothest, not a big one, but rising so perfectly to dusty white midges, with such fastidious grace, I felt honored just to share a seat at the same table.

I was wading a little deeper out into the current to try and see if I couldn't cover him with less drag, when I heard something upstream and to my right — heard it the way you hear a skyrocket going off, first in the gut, then in the ears. Recovering, jolted, I realized what I'd heard was a tremendous splash — a splash that resolved itself into outspreading ripples almost seismic in their velocity.

My first reaction was the skeptical one — some kid had thrown a rock. But there was no kid, only some innocent-looking Holsteins a hundred yards back from the bank. I was wondering if something that loud could possibly be what I hoped it might be when the sound came again, perhaps not as explosive as the first time, but — in that narrow glen — sufficient to shatter apart what remained of my doubt.

A trout! and not just any trout, but the Queen of the White River, Miss Stockbridge herself. This was the chance I'd been waiting for all season. I immediately forgot about the feeding trout in front of me, waded clumsily past him toward the far bank, then — just before sinking — got control of myself and started plotting things out.

The fish, wily monster that she was, had stationed herself in a deep channel hard against the shady bank. I couldn't wade directly over but had to backtrack fifty yards, then ease my way up through the shallows until I came within range. I did this carefully, keeping my eye on the spot the sound had come from, but — damn! A dicey spot made me glance away for a moment just as the fish splashed again.

I looked up, and this time managed to spot the epicenter of the rings, the place the fish had surfaced. It was within casting range — a long cast, but makeable. I was fishing a Light Cahill, and it made sense to stick with that. I tied a few more half hitches into my blood knot, then — my hands shaking — worked out line.

First cast — nothing.

Second cast — nothing.

Third cast — my God! I brought my arm up in a reflex motion, literally gasped from the force of striking, and clenched my teeth waiting for the monster's weight to come tight against the line.

Nothing happened.

Five minutes went by.

"Trout?" I felt like saying. "O trout? Are you there, trout?"

I was so surprised to have missed, so speechless, the disappointment in my stomach was so sudden and cold, that I didn't even try casting again, but bulled my way through the current to the place she had rose, trying to at least get a glimpse of what I had missed.

I was there looking down into the water when she rose again, this time so close it made me jump. I spun around, and was just in time to see, splashing into the water at my back, a beautifully ripe, beautifully crimsoned McIntosh apple, dropping from the highest branch of the outspreading apple tree that shaded the lie. Again, I glanced down into the water. There they were, bobbing just beneath the surface — splashes one, two, and three. I scooped one out and took a vicious bite of its middle, determined to have my vengeance on something's flesh. I understood immediately the ludi-crousness of what had happened; it's hard enough to be had by a trout, but to be had by a McIntosh apple?

That was yesterday. Now, looking back from the per-spective of my typewriter, I have only one regret — that the apple didn't hit me on the head. It worked, after all, for Newton, and God knows he was *not* a gullible man.

The Bigger They Come

My friends know me as a man who likes to exaggerate, but for the next five thousand words I'll stick to a sober recitation of the facts, the better to deal with events that are themselves sufficiently exaggerated. What I'm referring to are the two most extraordinary fish of my angling career, the first extraordinary for the circumstances of its capture, the second, for the circumstances of its capture and the extraordinariness of its size.

There are two schools of thought on catching big fish. One school holds that you fish for them deliberately, use outsize lures and streamers, fish only those lies capable of sheltering fish of weight. The second maintains the best way to catch big fish is to work your way through as many lesser fish as possible, harness the laws of probability to your cause. This last may be called the lottery school of fly-fishing, and it's the one to which I belong, since it pretty well matches what I've learned of life. The big things come unex-

pectedly amid the ordinariness of daily routine, and to deliberately go hunting Joy or Love with a metaphoric net would
be to doom yourself to failure by the very nature of the
quest. No, I'm a small-fish fisher, a small-fate man, who
hopes, like we all do, for miraculous things.

But this by way of preface. From here on in I'll adhere to
the Joe Friday school of angling literature: the facts, ma'am,
just the facts.

It wasn't meant to be a fishing trip at all. Nova Scotia for
two weeks — a trip we could manage with our baby. That I
packed a small fly rod was of no significance; it goes into my
duffle bag the automatic way my razor does; it wouldn't
matter if my destination were Bahrain. That Nova Scotia has
some fine fishing is something I was aware of, of course, but
that only added a vaguely illicit interest I wasn't going to
allow myself to pursue.

Nova Scotia is not your undiscovered, off-the-beaten-
track gem, but it's still lovely for all that; the descriptions
that speak of it as "Vermont surrounded by ocean," or "New
England thirty years ago," are both true. With its mix of
Acadian, Loyalist, and Scots traditions, its coastline that out-
craggys Maine's, and its laid-back Canadian citizenry, it's
the perfect spot for the kind of relaxed family vacation we
were after. Starting in Halifax, we were going to travel
around toward Cape Breton, staying at bed and breakfasts,
driving in the morning, hiking and picnicking in the
afternoon.

Our first night was spent near the Saint Marys, a famous
salmon river, but only because it's where we happened to be
when evening caught up to us. And though I may have
briefly entertained the notion of trying a cast or two, the

south-coast rivers were already closed for the season, the
victims of a summer-long drought that was the worst on
record. Still, after we settled in, there was no reason not to
stroll over to the river and have a look-see; our landlady told
us about a bald eagle who made his home in a spruce above
the iron bridge, and we wanted to try and spot him.

The facts — and yet already a digression. My attitude
toward salmon, to this point in my life, could pretty well be
summed up by the term *reverse snobbery*. Yes, I knew about
the mystique — about how Atlantic salmon were the king
of game fish, strong, brave, beautiful, and scarce; of Lord
Grey of Falloden and Edward Ringwood Hewitt and Lee
Wulff and Ted Williams, and all the famous fly-fishers who
dedicated their lives to its pursuit. And yes, I knew about
the efforts of conservationists not only to preserve the
salmon in their present range, but to bring them back to the
New England rivers they once inhabited. I even, God forgive
me!, knew what it was to carve into a side of smoked salmon,
curl off a piece and drop it on rye bread with a whisper of
onion, wash it down with good Danish beer. I knew all these
things, which isn't bad for a man who hadn't, until this
moment, seen an Atlantic salmon that was actually alive.

The reverse snobbery? Well, weren't all salmon fishers
rich bastards who mouthed pieties about protecting the fish
(protecting them, that is, from fishermen whose bank
accounts weren't as large as theirs), while back at work they
were presidents of corporations that were despoiling the
environment as fast as possible? And even the local effort to
return salmon to New England rivers — wasn't that a mis-
use of scarce conservation dollars, trying to bring something
so fragile back to a region where fish and game laws still

reflected the ethos of the Eighteenth Century? Just before our trip a man had been arrested for catching and killing one of the first Atlantic salmon to make it all the way up to the White River in Vermont; the man had been previously charged with beating his wife, and was to shoot himself before he could be brought to trial for killing the salmon. In a bizarre kind of way it all fit in — the violence done the salmon, the violence done to man. No mystique for me, thank you — when it came to my attitude toward salmon, I was very skeptical and confused.

At least until that walk along the Saint Marys. We found the eagle fast enough — he was soaring in a spiral from bank to bank, with the majestic, disdainful quality all eagles possess. We stood on the bridge trying to get our daughter to share in the excitement — "See, Erin? See nice pretty eagley?" — when fifty yards upstream there was a splashing sound with an odd uplift to it, as if someone were throwing rocks *out* of the water. I forgot about the eagle, and shifted my focus to a lower plain. There it was again, and this time there was no mistaking the fluid, bright shape that appeared a second before the splashing sound and disappeared a second before its echo.

Salmon! In the drought-ravaged river, they were in the one pool big enough to shelter them, and seemed — when we balanced our way along the bank to it — not overly concerned by their plight. The water was deep and dark enough that it was hard to make them out, at least until they jumped. They went straight up in the air then, and it was so sudden and joyous our hearts lifted with them, so we laughed out loud at their sheer exuberance. There were no falls there, no dams — if anything, they seemed to be

jumping out of the depths of their contentment, as if
remembering in intervals they *were* salmon and were
expected to do so for our delight.

By the time it was too dark to watch any longer, I was, if
not converted to the mystique, at least firmly in the salmon's corner as a devoted fan. Unlike other big fish I'd seen,
I was not immediately possessed by the desire to be attached
to one; it was subtler, more a wanting to be *around* them,
the way people swim with dolphins.

Next morning we stopped briefly to see if the salmon
were still there; if they were, they weren't jumping, and we
contented ourselves with another good look at the eagle.
Later in the morning was the restored village of Sherbrooke,
then beautiful, lonely Wine Cove, and then our trip was
fully in gear, and we made our way in a back-and-forth looping toward Cape Breton and the dramatic headlands of that
coast.

The weather, with the drought, was gloriously sunny and
hot. Here on the watersheds flowing into the Gulf of Saint
Lawrence the salmon season was still open, though the rivers looked just as low and hopeless as they had in the south.
I thought about fishing, went so far as purchasing a license,
but between my flimsy trout rod, a few battered trout flies,
and a wife and child, it seemed better to concentrate on the
hiking and beachcombing we could all do together.

And then I got my chance — at some brook trout fishing.
We were passing the Cheticamp River, a beautifully clear
stream flowing seaward from some bread-loaf–shaped hills a
short way above the Acadian town of the same name. It was
a hot Sunday afternoon, half of Cape Breton seemed to be
out enjoying the sunshine, and we had already stopped in a
roadside store for the makings of a picnic. Leaving our car

at the campground, we slipped Erin into the backpack, then started through the dappled sunlight of the old woods road that parallels the river's bank.

The first salmon pool is a forty-minute walk in from the road, and this is where we decided to stop — *not* because of the salmon (the river was too low to think about that) but because the granite ledge that shelved down into the pool was a perfect spot for a picnic. While things were readied, I waded down below the pool to the only fast water in sight. I was wading wet — in that heat, it was the only comfort available — and I had nothing stronger than my feather-weight pack rod — perfect for seeking out the small brook trout I hoped to find.

Small fish, small fly. I was tying on a number-fourteen Royal Wulff when behind me in the pool was a tremendous splash, as if someone had just dove headfirst off the ledge. I spun around, startled, and was just in time to see my wife pointing down toward the pool with what can only be described as an expression of total dumbstruck awe. Any doubt about what had caused the sound disappeared instantly — again, there was a tremendous splash, only this time at the center of it, breaking the pool's surface, becoming detached from it, hanging there like the froth of a silver geyser, hanging there for what seemed like minutes, hanging . . . hanging . . . tilting . . . falling . . . knifing back in, was a . . .

"Salmon!" we yelled, simultaneously.

The salmon was jumping, not rolling — I was told later a jumping salmon will never take a fly. But I was too inexperienced to know this; my hands shaking, I finished tying on the fly, added two more half hitches, then waded the six or seven steps to the lip of the pool. The salmon had come

up seventy feet away — a heroic cast for a little rod — but
I was afraid coming any closer would frighten him off. I
worked out line as quickly as I could, then — David with a
slingshot — let the fly shoot forward in what was undoubtedly the longest, luckiest cast of my life.

The fly landed perfectly, its tail pert on the water, its
hackles puffed and upright. There was barely any current in
the pool, so it floated back toward me slowly, my emotions
traveling with it in the classic emotional pattern of a drift —
anticipation and alertness flowing imperceptibly toward
disappointment as the fly came back untouched. Not on this
cast, I decided, but just as the thought formed there was a
saucer-sized dip in the water below the fly, then something
yearning up toward it, and faster than my thoughts could
operate, my rod arm was high above me and with an amazing, exhilarating tightening — a tightening with a *bottom*
to it — the salmon was on.

I reacted very coolly to this: I shouted "Holy fuck!" and
immediately fell down.

But even reduced to a state of blithering idiocy, there was
a surer instinct at work, and the tight arc in the rod never
softened, even as I thrashed my way to my feet. The fight
that ensued lasted nearly a half hour, and while there wasn't
a moment during that time I wasn't terrified the salmon
would break off, I also knew, in the strange contradiction
only fishermen will understand, that I *had* him, and unless
I blundered badly the fish was mine.

For even with that toy rod, the odds were all in my favor.
With the water so low, there was no way the salmon was
going to leave the pool, which was fine with me, since I had
no backing on my reel, and had already proved my inability

to chase after him. Our fight consisted of short, strong runs wherein the salmon proved he could take line out anytime he wanted, and continued stubborn pressure on my part, proving I was not without power myself. With the rod being so light, the tippet so frail, the exact ratio between the salmon's force and my force was delicately balanced, and if there was any skill involved it was the adjustment and readjustment needed to keep the equation constant.

After each surge, I managed to get the salmon closer, to the point where I could see him now, angled down in the crystal green water of the pool, the fly right in his jaw where it should be, his flanks a buttered silver color, his tail powerful and square. He was a good fish, not a huge one, but not a grilse either, and I estimated his length at over two feet. Up on shore my wife and baby were cheering me on, only they had been joined now by another forty people at least. Picnickers, bikers, fishermen, hikers — the woods had been empty when I hooked the salmon, but now people were materializing from the trees as if summoned by bush telegraph, and they alternated between calling out advice to me and discussing among themselves the chances of the fish getting away. Here I wanted to be alone with the experience — my first salmon! — and I had a cheering section, and it made it all ludicrous somehow, the mob up on shore adding a harder tug I wasn't sure I could handle.

Between the lip of the pool and the granite shelf was a towel-sized patch of sand, and — netless — this is where I decided to try and beach the fish. Each time he came in, I brought him a bit closer, letting him get used to seeing the sand, not bothering him when he turned back toward the pool's center. I had learned the first time I fought a fish his size (see below) that a long battle becomes psychological as much as physical — exhausted, you become indifferent to the outcome, and you're apt to try and snap out of it by forcing the fish. I was fighting this temptation more than the fish now, and after about ten near approaches I decided enough was enough and pulled the salmon toward the sand as hard as I dared.

And, to my surprise, it worked — the salmon with hardly a protest slid himself up on the beach and lay still. There is no use trying to describe my emotions — anyone who has landed a big fish will know the mingled triumph and relief, and anyone who hasn't will find it impossible to imagine what a bizarre sick feeling it leaves in your gut. I was happy of course — I turned toward my audience and threw my arms up like a hockey player celebrating a goal — but almost immediately I was faced with a new problem, this one the thorniest yet.

What to do with the fish. During our fight I'd acted under the assumption I was going to release him unharmed — unharmed, that is, if he survived the acid buildup that causes so many released salmon to later die. If anything, this resolution became firmer as the fight wore on, since it seemed ridiculous to think of a fish that had come so far, past gill nets and trawlers and oil spills and so many other perils, dying at the hands of a picnicking vacationer.

The crowd, though, thought otherwise; all through the fight they were operating under the assumption I was going to not only keep the fish but eat him as well. It's hard to say how this feeling manifested itself, but it did, and though I've withstood my share of peer pressure in my day, this was about the most concentrated dose I was ever subjected to at once. These were local people, good Acadians, and the only logical destination for a migrating salmon was their pot. That didn't square with my own philosophy, but I was on their home ground, a visitor, only it was my fish, to do with what I pleased — wasn't it? Back and forth I went, and there were several times during the fight when I was tempted to deliberately snap the leader, disburden myself of this ethical dilemma.

The fish landed now, I was quickly running out of time. Keep him and maintain hero status with the crowd? Release him and keep the sense of my immaculate self? It would have taken Immanuel Kant to reason through this, but then I was saved by a man calling out from the hemlocks where the crowd was thickest.

"You have your salmon permit, don't you, mister?"

I had no such thing. There was an audible sign of disappointment with that — obviously, the fish would have to be put back before a warden arrived. Relieved, I took the fly out of the salmon's jaw and began working him back and forth through the water. Ten minutes later, when I released him, only my wife and daughter remained to watch.

But still, the news traveled fast. A few minutes later, when we were walking back down the path toward the campground, happy, hot, and tired, a man met us carrying an old steel fly rod with a huge automatic reel. He was small and wiry, and looked to be in his seventies; he had a pipe in his mouth and wore an old stocking cap, and there was something stooped in his posture that made you think he was portaging an invisible canoe.

"Are you the man who caught the salmon?" he asked.

I allowed as it was indeed me.

"Your first salmon?"

I nodded.

"On your first cast?"

I nodded again.

"On your first salmon river?"

"Well, yes," I said, and there's no describing the look of amazement and envy that came over the man's face.

"Mister," he said, his head sinking toward his chest as if the canoe had just gotten heavier. "I've been fishing this river for twenty-five years and never caught even *one*."

In the late 1970s, learning to write, single, broke, I spent the year making a slow counterclockwise progression between temporary homes. Cape Cod in the summers, stretching fall there until the pipes in my unheated cabin began to freeze, then — throwing manuscripts, typewriters, and fishing tackle into my Volkswagen — the winter renting various houses in the quiet hills of northwestern Connecticut. In between were periods of rest and recuperation at my parents' home in New York. One of these intervals was in November, and looking around for something to fill up my time, I decided upon a little trout fishing out in Suffolk County on Long Island's eastern end.

That Long Island — the ancestral home of concrete — even has trout fishing will come as a surprise to many. Back in the Nineteenth Century it was an unspoiled pastoral landscape of surpassing beauty, and among its delights was trout fishing of a very high order indeed. The early American fishing writer Frank Forester, in an appendix to a revised edition of *The Compleat Angler,* raved on and on about the delights of Island trout fishing.

Long Island has been for many years the Utopia of New York sportsmen . . . trout fishing still flourishes there and is

likely to flourish as long as grass grows and water runs . . .
it abounds in small rivulets, which, rising in the elevations
midway along the Island's length, make their way without
receiving any tributary waters into their respective seas . . .
the brook trout are found in abundance and in a degree of
perfection which I have seen equalled in no other waters
either American or British.

Poor Forester! He must be thrashing about in his grave
to see what man has wrought there, and yet in what can only
be described as a miracle, a fragment of this idyllic fishery
remains: the Connetquot River on the Island's south shore.
Located within a defunct private club, managed now by the
state, the beautifully clear Connetquot is a river I fished
often once upon a time, and I've never visited a place that in
its unspoiled perfection, its lost-world kind of atmosphere,
gave me such a sense of time suspended, the past regained.
If Proust were a fly-fisher, this would be his stream — it's
the madeleine of trout rivers, and I loved it very much.

The Connetquot is run, very sensibly, on the British beat
system. You call, make a reservation, then check in at the
gatehouse and select your stretch of water. In November,
the pressure falls off, and this particular day was so cold and
ominous I was the only fisherman who showed up; there
was a note tacked to the gatehouse door instructing anyone
who stumbled along to leave their five dollars in the box and
help themselves to the river. Swaddled in thermal underwear and sweaters, toting a thermos of tea and bourbon, I
did just that.

Past the gatehouse is the clubhouse, a weathered old
building that even abandoned suggests a kind of leisured ele-
gance, so you half expect Jay Gatsby to pull up in a shiny

Stutz roadster. It faces the lake where the Connetquot opens behind a small dam; the road crosses the dam, and on the abrupt downstream side is one of the best beats on the river: a broad pool flanked by a picturesque old mill. Unlike the water above the dam, the pool can be reached by sea-run browns, and I'd heard rumors about fish so big they were scarcely credible. Rumors — only back in the spring, crossing above the pool on my way upriver, a fisherman fighting a small trout asked me to hold the net for him, and as I dipped it in, a monstrous shape appeared from the pool's depths, took a swipe at the hooked trout, missed, and vanished back whence it had come.

There was no one fishing the pool, but I decided to save it for later. I hiked around the lake through the pitch pine forest, fished the stream above, and caught several decent rainbows. The weather, bad to begin with, now turned vile, with snow mixed in with sleet, and aside from what the frigid air and water were doing to my torso, there was the added inconvenience of having the guides of my rod freeze up, so that casting was like whipping slush.

I was a tougher fisherman in those days, but even so there were limits. Toward noon, I'd had enough, and started back toward the gatehouse. Walking helped warm me up — between this and the "one last cast" theory, I decided to fish the pool below the dam.

I went in on the left bank. It's an abrupt drop-off there, but being right-handed, fishing downstream, it would allow me to get the longest drift. The water comes into the pool in a heavy gray surge from the spillway, churns through the middle, then widens into the broad, placid tail. I tied on a brown Matuka, the New Zealand pattern that was all the rage, then, with the steep bank rising behind me, I roll cast out into the current and let the streamer swing down.

I hadn't been casting long when a brown caught hold of the Matuka and skittered across the pool toward me. He was small, and I was hardly paying any attention to bringing him in, when between one moment and the next the middle of the pool fell away, as if a petcock had suddenly been opened in the river bottom. But no — that simile isn't violent enough. As if a depth charge had gone off in the pool's center, so what I was aware of was the odd, backward sensation of seeing the water implode.

If the rise of that salmon on the Cheticamp was so measured and graceful it gave me time to see it all in slow motion, this was exactly the opposite experience — it happened so fast it's recorded in my memory as a bewildering blur. At about the same instant I realized something had slashed toward the trout I was playing — a rogue alligator? a misplaced shark? — my rod bent double and nearly snapped, and I remembered, with an emotion that nearly snapped *me* double, the monstrous trout that had frightened me back in the spring.

If it wasn't he, it was surely his brother — his *big* brother. I'd always heard browns turned cannibal when they reached the right size, and this was evidence of the strongest, most vicious sort. Engorged with the smaller trout, the brown turned toward the middle of the pool, giving me a good view of his huge, incredibly powerful tail — in turning, he left a shadow in the water that was part silver, part cream. That it was the largest trout I'd ever seen or even thought about was obvious at once; that I was attached to it seemed a hallucination.

Fight back, I told myself. Fight back! I was charged up
now, ready to follow him down through the marshes to the
Atlantic, but he hardly seemed concerned with what little
pressure I dared apply. He lived in the center of that pool
and in the center of that pool he was going to stay, and we
both knew my leader was too miserably light to do anything
about it. I thought about changing my stance, applying pressure from another direction, but with the bank so steep, the
drop-off so sudden, I was stuck. The best thing to do, at least
for the time being, was to stay where I was, keep the line
tight, and await developments.

These were not long in coming.

(Remembering my disclaimer at the beginning of this
essay, I write the following two paragraphs in the full
knowledge not a single one of my readers will believe them,
yet every word is true. The only thing I ask you to remember is how the laws of probability necessarily imply
the improbable — that a tossed penny, tossed frequently
enough, will eventually land on its edge.)

The trout was toward the middle, placid part of the pool,
deep, but not so deep I couldn't see him. There was no sign
of the smaller trout he had swallowed or the fly the smaller
trout had swallowed to start the chain off, yet my leader ran
straight down the big fish's mouth (I remember wondering
if, when it came time to brag of him, it would be more accurate to say I caught him on bait or the fly). My pressure,
light as it was, irritated him enough that he swung his head
around and started calmly back in my direction, thereby
changing the angle enough that the hook came loose.

I stripped in line furiously, unable to come to terms with
the fact the big trout was gone. Instinctively, doing it faster
than I write these words, I swung line, leader, and trout-

impaled fly back into the center of the pool. Again, the bottom of the water seemed to drop away, again the rod bent double, and not more than ten seconds after I lost him, the big trout — the big cannibalistic gluttonous suicidal trout — was on again.

There the two of us were, bound tight to each other in a swirl of frigid gray water, fish and man. The snow had dropped back again, stinging my eyes; my legs were numb from iciness, my arms all but palsied from the effort of holding the rod. A few yards away was the trout, bothered himself now, the hook embedded at an angle that must have plugged directly into his nervous system and hurt something essential, coming back to me with grudging reluctance, his thoughts filled with — what? Anger? Homesick memories of the ocean where he had spent his adolescence? Guilty reminiscences of all the smaller trout he must have eaten to obtain his weight? Or was his entire awareness centered in that sore, relentless ache in the jaw that meant his time was up? We swam in our misery together, danced our stubborn dance, and for upwards of an hour stayed attached in that partly sweet, oddly bitter symbiosis that is playing a fish of size.

The rest of the story doesn't take long to tell. Gradually, over the space of that hour, we were both weakening, and it was merely a question of who would reach exhaustion first. As in any epic of endurance, there were minor battles won and lost, various swings in the pendulum of fate, but twenty years later these have all been lost in the predominant, simplified memory of my tug versus the trout's.

Toward the end another fisherman appeared. With over forty beats on the river to choose from, he had reserved the pool by the dam, and he didn't act pleased to find me there.

He was a cool customer altogether; looking down from the spillway, he could see the trout quite clearly, but he hardly seemed impressed. I asked to borrow his net and he scaled it over to me, then, with a sullen expression, starting casting as if neither I nor the fish were there.

The trout was coming closer now, to the point I could start worrying about how to land him. The net was far too small to do the job, which left beaching him as the only alternative — beaching him, only there wasn't any beach. Behind me was the steep mud of the bank; to my right, the deep water near the dam; to my left, bushes and saplings that overhung the bank far enough to push me out over my head.

It was the bank then — that or my arms. I had the fish close to me now — he was so large I was shy of looking at him directly — and by increasing the pressure just a little I was able to swim him around so he rested between my waist and the bank. Coaxing my legs into motion, I waded in toward him, gradually narrowing the space he had left to swim, until there was less than a yard between him and shore. Again, there was no shelf here — it was like backing him against a wall. Finally, with a dipping, scooping motion, I got my arms under his belly, lifted him clear of the water . . . held him for a moment . . . then, just as I tensed my muscles prior to hurling him up the bank, watched helplessly as he gave that last proverbial flopping motion, broke the leader, and rolled back free into the pool from whence he came.

How did I feel? How would *you* feel? — that multiplied by ten. While obviously I never had the chance to put the fish on the scales, I'd had him in my arms for a few seconds, and kept a clear view of him for over an hour before that. I put his weight at eight pounds (no, I put it at *twelve* pounds, but I'm going to reduce it to cling to what credibility I have left, though reducing it is the only lie in this essay). An eight-pound brown trout — a fish that would be large for Argentina, let alone Long Island. I knew, with a feeling beyond words, that it was the biggest trout I would ever have a chance for, and that the rest of my angling career would be nothing but a futile search among lesser fish for his peer.

Melodramatic, perhaps, but I was slow to snap out of the bitter aftertaste losing him had left. In one sense I had landed the trout, if landing meant getting him out of the water into my arms, and in any case I'd decided during the midst of our fight to release him. There was some comfort in this, but when I shuffled my way out from the pool onto dry land, I was shaking with cold and stiffness and disappointment, and something even more intense I didn't believe existed until then: buck fever.

To be that close to something immense, to fight it for what from the trout's point of view was life or death, to have it and lose it in the very same instant — these were the ingredients tangled together at the emotion's core. But there was more that's harder to explain. It was as if during those minutes I was attached to him, all the civilized, dulling layers that separate me from my ancestral, elemental self — the hunter and gatherer that, reach back far enough, dwells in us all — had been tugged away, giving instinct its chance to romp through my nervous system in the old half-remembered patterns, so what I felt was the sick nauseous *human* emotion of a hunter at the end of the chase.

It didn't last very long, at least in one respect. In five minutes I was back at my car, dumping ice out of my waders, pouring the warm tea and bourbon directly over my toes. And yet a trace of that emotion lingers on to this day, as if the trout had been attached so long and fought so determinedly he welded a circuit between myself and that ancient, vaguely suspected self — the self that once fought giants and defeated a few and knew what disappointment was right down to the thrilling marrow of the bones.

October 15

To the river.

The leaves were blown down in a Columbus Day gale, and what foliage is left drifts just beneath the surface of the current like a separate soggy river of red and gold. Now, in the brilliant sunshine of the storm's passing, with no shade, the color is blinding, stronger off the water than at any time during the summer. But no — *off* is not quite the word. The brightness is *in* the water, as if the usual laws of reflection have been suspended, the sun taken in rather than mirrored, the subtlety washed out into something that is already closer to December's steel than to August's velvet. The sun is tossed up in the rapids and aerated, stirred out in the pools and cooled, turning even the most familiar lies into mysteries of impenetrable radiance, so — wading into all this, trying to get my bearings, flipping down my Polaroids — I immediately feel at a loss. Brightness to the left of me,

brightness to the right — it's as if the water has turned molten, and I have no idea where to cast. *When the radiance
gets into the water the fishing is over* — it's Wetherell's
Third Law of Fishing, and I try to take comfort from it, since
it's apparent in the way my line and fly disappear in the hard
beauty that this will be an afternoon without trout.

For all the times I've fished the river, there are stretches
I still haven't tried. This is one of them — a quarter mile of
riffles and pools backing the overgrown acreage of a newly
abandoned farm. It's the classic New England scene, of
course. Stone walls choked with briars, a rusty thresher
obscured in milkweed, the ungrazed fields going back to ivy
and birch. Up on a knoll is the abandoned farmhouse and
barn, the boards already sagging into a closer, snugger fit to
the land, though it's only a month since the last struggling
farmer failed there and moved on. New England's landscape,
at its purest, has a genius for nature's soft reclamation —
ashes turn to ashes nowhere prettier than here.

There are stories in all this — it's the classic New England literary landscape as well. Ruined dreams, vanished villages, the bittersweet suggestion of an apple tree growing
beside an old cellar hole — these have been the staples of
the region's fiction through Frost and Jewett and Wharton
and Howells all the way back to Hawthorne, whose genius
not only captured the lonely shadows over these hills but
cast his own that lingers in our imaginations to this day.
Many talented writers have worked this terrain; many talented writers work it still, mopping up the tragic left-
overs — the last farmers struggling to stay afloat; the irony
of a flinty land dying through prosperity — though it's clear
that here as the Twentieth Century lurches and stumbles its
way toward a finish, New England has become a literary

backwater, and its writers of fiction will have to turn their attention outward from our old familiar parish if they are to avoid total irrelevancy. Me, when I see the birches I think of Russia and copses and Tolstoy — my imagination glances off.

Fishing? No, but the kind of thing I'm apt to consider when I'm not catching fish. For all the perfection of the water behind the farm, despite the generosity of an afternoon that gives me, in quick succession, sights of hawks, grouse, mink, vultures, and deer (plus a rarity, a turtle sunbathing in the stream!), it's obvious my first instinct was right — that I could change from using a Gold-Ribbed Hare's Ear to TNT and still catch nothing.

The realization that you will be skunked is one of the hardest things in the fishing life; when in the day that moment comes is one of the diciest timings. Sometimes the signs are so ominous you know with the first cast you're going to strike out all day; other times, conditions are so ripe you can work for hours, and, fishless, still feel certain your next cast will bring a rise. I've had my share of both experiences, particularly the former. In September, just before leaving for an overnight trip to the upper Connecticut, I was met with the following weather report: "The eye of Hurricane Hugo will pass over Pittsburg, New Hampshire (our destination!), sometime during the morning Saturday, bringing torrential rain, followed by an Arctic cold front that will leave up to six inches of snow by Sunday morning." Maybe it's the pessimist in me, but I had a strong presentiment — subsequently confirmed — that it was not going to be a trip rich in trout.

There was one obscure period in my life when I used to venture into singles bars; I remember the disappointment that came, usually with the third vodka and tonic, when I swallowed the fact I would be leaving alone. A similar disappointment is what I'm talking about here; we put so much behind us when we go fishing, work, trivialities, worries, that, with disappointment, we risk having it all flood back. That the fish isn't everything, that it's enough merely being outside surrounded by beauty, up to our waists in living water, is certainly true, of course, but it's amazing how much truer it seems if we've caught at least one trout. Fishless, the temptation is to fish longer than conditions warrant, thereby setting up a vicious cycle — the longer you fish without a fish, the more you need one; the more you need one, the more your disappointment grows; the longer you fish, et cetera, et cetera.

Fly-fishers differ in nothing so much as they do this, the willingness to admit defeat. It's one of the trickiest things in a fishing friendship, the fatalist ready to throw in the towel too quickly, the optimist fishing far beyond hope's outer bound. The best partnerships work out a code to face facts gently . . . "Anything doing down your way? . . . What do you make of this cold front? . . . Does that store down the road sell Molson's?" . . . and with mutual commiseration agree the moment has come to transfer hope to the next day out, take down the rods, and quit.

Alone, it's a harder decision for me, since it means not only ending the day, but the season. Between the empty brightness of the water (my thermometer measures it as forty-nine degrees), my fishless conviction, the sense of regret and finale suggested by the abandoned farm, my thoughts change focus, so somewhere between the log-sheltered pool at the start of the run and the undercut bank at the finish, I've turned from hoping what the next cast will bring to remembering what the long season has brought.

A good year, I decide — no monsters, but even so. There was the spring when I finally got the hang of fishing a nymph; a June morning when I caught two dozen smallmouth, the slightest of which was two pounds; the discovery of a secret brook trout stream no wider than a sidewalk; the start of some new fishing friendships (to this habitual loner, a miraculous thing); the rediscovery of my river after a year of drought and too long a time away.

The season was over; as they say in Hollywood, "That's a wrap," and then as I turned to climb up onto the bank a brown trout tugged on my trailing Muddler, re-creating for the time he was on the hope I had already given up. But what was odd, as careful as I handled things, it hardly seemed like I was playing him in the present tense at all, but off in the future somewhere — that beautiful as he was, he was pulling at me from April of the coming year, so at last, when I landed him on the rocks, knelt down, and released him, I was faced the right way for winter, with the right spirit, with just enough hope to pamper toward spring.

Why Fish?

I have an uncle for whom I have a great deal of affection, despite the fact we have very little in common. Over the years, by default, most of our conversations have been about his bowling, the only subject I've ever found that will take us past the uncomfortable silence after preliminary remarks about weather and health have quickly been exhausted. People need a tag, a quick label, to make it easy for insensitive dullards like myself to work up some chitchat. Mine — now that the tables have been turned and I'm an uncle myself, with nieces and nephews faced with the daunting prospect of making me talk — is fishing. "So, how's the fishing been, Walter?" — this in lieu of asking me about my latest novel, or the condition of my back, or all those murky, complicated things that might, with unpredictable consequence, get me started.

So I tell them — so I tell you — that by and large the fishing has been very good, thank you. A balm and supportive to the soul, an antidote to bitterness, a relief and a restorative and a reward. What I don't tell them, though I'm tempted to, is that I'm going to quit it any day now and take up bowling myself.

It's amazing, now that I think of it, how much time I spend dreaming, not about fishing, but about *quitting* fishing — of selling off my tackle at a tag sale, ripping up my waders to use as chaffing around our fruit trees, donating my fishing books to a responsible charity, turning my canoe into a planter. For all the gentleness of the sport, it has the maddening trick of suddenly turning on you, becoming a burr and an irritant, a breeder of bitterness, a plague and a problem and a pox.

These manic attitude swings have been a feature of my fishing right from the start. I remember once as a fourteen-year-old being deposited by my parents near a river that was said to have monstrous bass, and being picked up again in tears four hours later, driven to despair by the dozen lures I had lost on the brush-choked bottom, the wet clay I had foundered in, the sweat that poured over my face, the branches that knocked off my glasses, the terrible disappointment of catching, for all my agony, absolutely naught. Even closer than that, even yesterday. After three days of rain, three days of being locked in the house, I was desperate to go fishing, to the point where I talked myself into believing the rivers wouldn't be flooded, though I knew in the suppressed half of me they would be exactly that. Forty miles later, arrived at the river I had inexplicably chosen, I saw the situation was exactly as I foresaw: the river was over its banks and unfishable. Nothing daunted, I drove on to another river, fooling myself into thinking it hadn't rained as much over there; that river, of course, turned out to be flooded, too, and there I was at eight in the evening a hundred miles from home, exhausted, disappointed, and so mad at myself I feared for my sanity.

As unnerving as this type of thing can be, it's the natural downside of anything that is pursued passionately over any length of time. If worse comes to worst and I give in to my peevish irritation, make good my threat to quit, no one will be the loser except for me. But it's one thing to give up something cherished through your own free will, quite another to have something cherished taken away from you by force.

Let me backtrack here to an incident that happened this summer. I was teaching at a writer's conference, feeling, as you do at these things, that I was a minnow of some small knowledge pursued by voracious muskellunge hungry for same. To escape, I went fishing. A few miles from the campus is a surprisingly good trout stream, replete with pools and riffles that stay cold even in July. I fished it regularly for a week, got into some nice browns each morning (including a monster that broke off during a thunderstorm I had no right being out in — but that's another story), enjoyed some Vermont scenery at its most pastoral, and in general had a delicious time. On the seventh day, though the water was just as perfect and clear, I caught nothing. Walking back to my car, puzzled, I saw a highway crew leaning over a bridge downstream of the stretch I'd fished; they had long-handled nets with them, and were leaning over the water to scoop up dead, colorless trout, tossing them into their truck as if they were cans of Budweiser thrown there by slobs.

The explanation wasn't long in coming. A valve had been turned the wrong way at the municipal swimming pool six miles upstream, releasing chlorine and other chemicals into the river, killing upwards of fifteen thousand fish — demonstrating, among other things, how even the clearest trout stream is nothing more than another pipe in our municipal waste system; one twist of the dial and trout, mystique, and purity are all flushed away.

Now it seems to me this episode is both a perfect literal description and a perfect metaphor for the present condition of American trout fishing. There I was fishing that gloriously pristine river, oblivious to the fact the water that shined so brilliantly was in reality poisoned — that the browns I had caught earlier in the week and released so carefully were now being hauled off to the dump. We cherish our traditions, do the best we can to leave no imprint on the stream, and despite our best efforts the water is dying anyway, to the point where we realize how pathetic the enterprise has become, and fish less often, and eventually find excuses not to face this irony at all.

People whose backs are against the wall, pressed hard enough, will eventually lash out with their fists, and if there's any good news to be had in the depressing roll call of environmental catastrophe, it is this: that lovers of nature, fly-fishers among them, are beginning to fight back. I have a friend who spends many hours each week working on behalf of Trout Unlimited, traveling around the country spreading their message of wise and measured use of our fishery resources. I have another friend who puts his talents as a lawyer to use in suing those who would dam and harness every molecule of moving water they can find. Still another friend, while having neither the time nor temperament to work so aggressively, goes out of his way to contribute money to conservation organizations, and isn't shy about lambasting senators, representatives, and wardens for the primitive fishing regulations still in effect. I have another friend — a real favorite — who does none of these things, but fights underground, pouring syrup into the tanks of bulldozers he comes upon deep in the forest, ripping out survey stakes, and in general making good use of those monkey-wrenching tactics made famous by the late, great Edward Abbey.

There are those who would shake their heads at my last friend, counsel moderation, but I am not one of them. It is clear, after a century of lip service to "conservation" matched by environmental disasters of unparalleled scope, that the time has come for those who care for natural beauty to think in terms of revolution, consider using the guerrilla hit-and-run tactics that are a prelude to any full-scale revolt. While it's certain the bulk of measurable results are being garnered by friends one and two, supported by the dollars of friend three, it's equally clear it's time to start adopting the tactics of friend four, to see whether civil disobedience might not be more effective. The environmental movement needs its radical left, and not only that, but a radical right, an organization that would fight with the same fanatic devotion for the fish lobby (with over seventy-five million fishermen on this continent, how formidable it would be!) with the same fanatic devotion as the NRA fights for the gun lobby.

Me, I've torn down my share of survey ribbons in my day, finding the little shredding tug as they come apart to be among nature's most delightful sensations. But still, at my age, in my circumstances, I haven't yet grown into the radical I aspire to become when my courage matures. Those who write of nature in this country are given a different task: to carefully explain what it is in beauty that is worth saving, and thereby give those who fight in the trenches a clearer sight of what they defend.

Add that to the list of devastation wrought by developers and highway builders and politicians and our own wasteful sloth: that even someone who writes about something as innocent as fishing must adopt the vocabulary of apocalypse and confrontation, deviate as far from the pastoral style of a Charles Cotton — patron saint of fly-fishing — as our threatened streams differ from his untroubled Dove. To be written honestly in this day and age, a fishing book has to acknowledge the threats squarely, or hide behind a nostalgic obscuration — has to take on an edge, as it were, and sacrifice a portion of its lyricism to the hard blade of truth.

A portion — but not all. If nothing else in this book, I hope I've conveyed the delights fly-fishers can find in the practice of their incredibly simple, incredibly sophisticated art. Here at the end it seems appropriate to be quite explicit about what prompts me to spend a good portion of half the year trying to convince trout and bass and pike the bauble I am floating across their narrow cone of vision is in reality a morsel of food — to make, as an affirmation of faith, a list of the reasons I fish. For convenience, I will separate out the constituent motives, and not only that, try to rank them in order of personal importance, but only with the disclaimer that in fishing, like life, everything comes in one overwhelming jumble, lists and categories be damned.

Why, then, fish?

1. *Geographic discovery*

A real surprise for starters, a very personal reason, and one I didn't appreciate the force of until I sat down to make this list. Simply stated, the prime motivation for my fishing is to explore rivers, lakes, oceans, and ponds — explore them, in my small way, like La Salle or Champlain or one of those early explorers whose eyes had first crack at this continent; explore with a global kind of curiosity the small hidden corners of the world.

In practice, this works on two modest levels: my continually wanting to try new rivers, not so much to discover whether they have any fish, but simply to see where they *go;* my returning again and again to familiar water, to explore it a little further, try that pool that's always been a little too remote. The first has resulted in many happy discoveries of places I would never have seen without fishing as my ostensible purpose (for instance, the wild scrub forest of Cape Cod, which I stumbled into in my pursuit of its elusive salter trout); the second, in my continual amazement at how the familiar can yield so much that is brand-new (yesterday on the Waits, again stumbling, I came upon a small tributary that doesn't appear on any map).

I have a deep curiosity about land and waterscape, which, trace it back far enough, probably has something to do with the infant Wetherell's delight in exploring the steadily expanding boundaries of cradle, bassinet, nursery, and yard. It's almost impossible to exaggerate the adult dimensions of this delight; I want to swallow terrain whole, sink my teeth into it, so when I travel, even to a stream half a mile away, I'm possessed by a restlessness and curiosity that both propels me and leaves me drained. It has another, sadder effect: it makes me a much worse fisherman than I would be if I could linger with more patience. Sure the trout are rising right there in the pool ahead of me, but what is that compared to the allure of the canyon or waterfall that might be around the next bend?

Closely allied to geographic discovery is the exploration of time; indeed, it would be more accurate to speak of the space-time continuum in all the above. Time of day is one of the things a fisherman learns best, in all its subtle shading, from that first riverine curl of gray in the east that comes before true dawn, to the slow clockwise spin of the Great Bear over a bass lake in total dark. Even here I can tune the list finer: of all the times of day, it is dusk — summer dusk — that interests me most, and I often go fishing simply to immerse myself in some, let its settling curtain bring the gentle shadows and increasing stillness I love so well.

2. A role in the natural world

Going fishing to be "outside," going fishing to see "nature." These are familiar explanations for something more subtle, the compelling reason I put second on my list, but which could equally be first. In this industrialized age of ours, man — only a few generations removed from coaxing his living from the farm, the forest, or the water — is sick to death because of the artificial divisions he has established between himself and the natural world. Anything that gets us past these divisions is worthy of passionate pursuit, whether it be the flowers of the suburban gardener or the birds of the amateur ornithologist.

What is special about fishing in general and fly-fishing in particular is that the pursuit of fish alone, with no other object in view, brings with it all kinds of attendant marvels, from sights of hawks and ospreys and foxes, to the more intimate miracles of tiny wildflowers and insects that to anyone but a fly-fisher and a trout would be invisible (I think of Thoreau's phrase, "All this is apparent to the observant

eye, but would pass unnoticed by most"). Just being outside
in nature is not as good a means of discovering nature as it
is to *ask* something of it; we have to pose specific questions
to nature for it to answer; we have to sharpen our senses to
search for trout, and, sharpened, those senses are available
to take in the mysteries our duller selves would miss.

But to put the motivation more clearly, I can do no better
than to quote the naturalist Henry Beston. Asked what
understanding he gained from his year alone in the "outer-
most house" on the dunes of Cape Cod, he replied: "I would
answer that one's first appreciation is a sense that the crea-
tion is still going on, that the creative forces are as great and
active to-day as they have ever been, and that to-morrow's
mornings will be as heroic as any in the world." This at
some level is what every fisherman learns when he spends
time on the water, and the spirit of this in our pessimistic
age is intoxicating and one of the prime reasons that makes
us fish.

3. Tactileness

There's almost nothing that feels as good against the skin
as water, which is what all those beaches and water slides
and hot tubs and pools and showers and bathtubs are all
about. Even the most sedentary bait fisher will dangle his
bare toes over the rowboat to establish contact with its coolness, and one of the consistent delights of fly-fishing is to be
immersed in this element at varying depths. It's a hard pleasure at times, to be sure; to stand chest deep in an April river
slightly over freezing is something only a masochist would
find pleasure in, but even here, the numbness in the body
creates a sharpness in the mind, and lets you know, as few
other tingles can, that you are alive.

But usually it's much better than that. A May river on the back of one's legs, cooling pleasantly through the wader fabric, supporting by its force, lightening by its buoyancy — if there's anything as sensuously rich it's only the same river in July, when the waders are gone and the current comes directly against bare legs. Add to this a breeze against the neck, a fishing breeze from the south carrying with it the earthy damp of fiddlehead ferns, the slippery firmness of a trout against the palm, the dust of mayflies blowing against your cheek during a good hatch, the pleasant, loosening tug on the shoulders caused by casting . . . there can be few pastimes that in their normal execution feel as good as this.

4. Fish

Anyone who's come this far with me will know I admire fish greatly, spend a great deal of time longing to be connected to one, study their habits and habitat with a good deal of attention, and the only thing to do here is explain why I haven't listed them first on my list. For me, the fish is not the be-all and end-all of the fishing process, though I feel like the Mad Hatter in writing this down. I have an intense curiosity about fish, but it has its limits, while the first three listings come without bounds.

That fish are hard animals to love (love, say, like I love swallows) will come as no surprise to anyone who thinks about it; their cold-blooded status creates a barrier our mammalian solipsism finds difficult to bridge. Then, too, they are quarry; to even the most sophisticated of anglers, the strictest conservationist, the most devoted catch-and-releaser, they are *quarry*, something hunted, and while respect, insight, and empathy can flourish in the hunting process, it's a perversion of the term to speak of love. No matter what fishing represents to us, to fish it's a grim life-and-death struggle, and though I've caught my share of fish that winked at me, I've never seen one that smiled.

I have a passion for fishing, a lesser passion for the fish themselves. But passion is passion, and if fish aren't first in my motives, they are still high up there on the chart. If catching fish involved none of the first three entries, but meant instead you had to wade foul urban alleys beset by rats, I would still pursue them intently. Land a good trout or bass, hold it for a second on the wet skin of your hand, and you have, in one compact bundle, as beautiful and bewildering a combination of opposites as it's possible to imagine; strength and litheness, fragility and toughness, intelligence and obtuseness, fastidiousness and voraciousness, boldness and stealth. And even if you're not as fond of contradictions as I am, what other creature comes close to a fish in color and fluid grace? Offered a shot at reincarnation, I would opt for being a trout without any hesitation at all — a wild twelve-inch brook trout, say, at home in a small brook that made me slightly bigger than my peers, living out my days with detachment and a certain world-weary wisdom that would perfectly complement my size.

Perhaps I would be a better fisherman if I didn't admire fish so greatly; I've never been able to turn them completely into objects, never been willing to apply any science to them, preferring, like the stars, that they swarm about me with their mysteriousness intact.

5. Texture of memory

Number five now, but climbing higher with each year. More and more I fish to reestablish contact with places, times, and events I have in memory; so present fishes for past, as it were, and when a memory takes hold hard its current flows up the line and lives in all its intensity again. Fifteen years ago, this wasn't the case — I simply hadn't fished long enough, my experiences were too scattered to take on any texture. It takes five or more years' fishing the same water under a variety of conditions to create a dense enough association that your fishing becomes enriched; fishing the Waits, I think of the young man I was ten years ago wading into the same river without knowing where any of its trout were, hardly knowing where to look; fishing Franklin Pond above my home, I think of springs a decade in the past when I caught trout that even now stand out vividly enough in my recollection that I can picture every spot. The time my wife bailed a leaky rowboat three inches from swamping, while I, sitting oblivious in the stern, fought and landed a five-pound largemouth; the patient way my mother used to take me fishing at our Connecticut summer home when my father was working; a slow, lazy trip down a bass river with two good friends, eating carrot cake on a sandbar under a warm summer rain. I remember these hardly ever when I'm not fishing — it takes being on a reminiscent body of water, fishing in a similar evening light, to bring the memory back, and this explains the allure of familiar water, the reason we never tire of it though we fish it again and again.

6. *Literature and tradition*

Saint Peter, Dame Julian Berners, Leonard Macall, Gervase Markham, Izaak Walton, Charles Cotton, Sir Edward Grey, George M. L. La Branche, G. E. M. Skues, Edward

Ringwood Hewitt, Theodore Gordon, Dolly Varden, William Scrope, J. W. Hill, Huck Finn, Plunket Greene, Patrick Chalmers, H. T. Sheringham, John Burroughs, Queequeg, Eugene Connet, John Taintor Foote, Eric Taverner, Preston Jennings, Ernest Hemingway, Zane Gray, Caroline Gordon, the Darbees, A. W. Miller, Odell Shephard, Robert Traver, Nick Lyons, Norman Maclean, Arnold Gingrich, Ed Zern, Roderick L. Haig-Brown, Pogo, Red Smith, Angus Cameron, Ted Hughes, Elizabeth Bishop, Lee Wulff, Charles Ritz, Paul Young, Charles Fox, William Humphrey, Vincent Mariano, et al.

7. Art and craft

Art is not a word to toss around lightly, and it's important to remember fly-fishing is not an art in the same way painting the Sistine Chapel is, or writing *The Charterhouse of Parma*. The kind of patience a fisherman needs is similar to that of the artist — a passionate, active patience, the kind that knows when to search and when to wait — and of course imagination and talent also play their part. The *art* of fly-fishing, though, leans more toward the *craft* side of the term; we speak of the art of holding a runner on first base, the art of putting, the art of fishing a size-twenty-eight midge, when the word *craft* would work better. Fly-fishing differs from most sports in the almost infinite variety of art-crafts that come into play even routinely. There's the art of fine rod making, the art of fly-tying (here if anywhere the word art means ART), the art of casting, the art of reading a river, the art of hooking a trout in fast water, the art of playing a heavy fish.

Fly-fishing is enough like art that aesthetic satisfaction is an important ingredient when you total up its delights.

What's more, there's a mechanical satisfaction that comes from the execution of perfect technique, the intellectual satisfaction that is similar to solving a hard chess problem, the athletic satisfaction that — with the hand-eye coordination involved in casting — is similar to shooting baskets. When things go right, that is. What a day on the river usually becomes is an amalgam of mechanical triumph and mechanical fiasco, aesthetic disaster and aesthetic bliss, and it's this dizzying roller coaster that resembles art most of all, so defeat is there in all our minor victories, victory there in all our major defeats.

8. Toys

It's hard not to get carried away here. Is there any adult pastime that brings with it such a delightful treasure chest of toys as fly-fishing? Reels that go clickety-clackety-clack, rods that whip the air about and magically extend our reach, waders we go clomping around in, hooks adorned with feathers (feathers of guinea hen, fur of polar bear, tinsel from a Christmas tree!), little springy things, pastes and scissors and sharp instruments our mothers would have in no circumstances let us touch . . . the playroom was never as good as this.

Fishing tackle brings us back to the days when our only work was play, our toys the means by which we explored our limited and infinite world. Toys, and yet there's more to it than that; reels not only go clickety-clack, but purr exquisitely, and there are satisfactions in owning a fine bamboo fly rod that mimic the satisfactions in owning a Stradivarius; indeed, there are people who don't fish at all, but spend many hours and dollars assembling collections of rare rods and reels.

My own passion is for lures; I don't think there has been a time in my life when I wasn't enamored of one variety or another. When I was younger it alternated between River Run Spooks, those scoop-nosed, hook-festooned plugs that resemble aquiline minnows, and Jitterbugs, the platter-faced marvels I spent too much of my allowance on when I was twelve. Since turning fly-fisher, I've run through a whole parade of favorite flies: Muddlers, Honey Blondes, Brown Bivisibiles, Gray Fox Variants, Royal Wulffs. It's no exaggeration to say I can stare at a perfectly tied Royal Wulff for minutes at a time, delighting in the deer-hair puff of it, the crisp red and white color. Just the word lure is alone enough to fascinate me; how many lures of any kind does man have in his arsenal? and how many of those are as bright and purposeful as a number-sixteen dry fly?

There are fishermen who overdose on tackle; almost all do during some stage of their fishing career, and what is means can too easily become ends. Winter is the time to indulge this passion — late winter when the tackle companies are canny enough to send out their catalogs. Once the season comes it's best to simplify things as much as possible. Anyone who's been a kid knows the very best thing to do with toys is make a cache of them, a chest or drawer no one else can touch, and I advise the same for the novice fly-fisher; buy all you want, but when you go out to the river, leave all but the essential tackle at home and concentrate your passion on the fish.

9. Solitude

In this day and age solitude runs to two extremes. To people who are locked in by it, unable to make contact with any human no matter how ardently they try, it must seem an evil spell they would do anything to shatter; to those caught up in the vortex, physically and psychologically hemmed in and supported by a network of friends, relatives, lovers, and colleagues, with all the mental battering that happily and unhappily results, solitude must seem an impossible dream, something longed for with just as much intensity as the lonely bring to its detestation.

So it's a condition to speak about carefully, lest its gate abruptly swing down and block our retreat. Suffice it to say that here in the industrialized West, solitude, spatial solitude and silence, is next to impossible to find; we retreat to our homes, but the television lies waiting; we try to find it in sleep, but outside the horns keep blaring, the sirens rush past. Fly-fishing for trout, done properly, requires much time alone on the stream; one of the few rules that seems to hold true in all circumstances is that the farther from the road you go, the better the fishing becomes. Countless times I've followed trout from pool to pool, catching one here, one there, until I've been led deep into the forest like Hansel and Gretel toward the witch's house, only it's a good witch this time, and, when I remember to break for lunch, I'm amazed at what silence I've managed to reach — how between one pool and the next the sounds of the mechanized world have dropped away and I'm as isolated and solitary as if I stood on a peak in the Hindu Kush.

But perhaps even this experience is too solitary and enchanted to speak of in print. Just say that being alone is a rare pleasure to those lucky enough not to be alone, and fly-fishing, notwithstanding entry number ten, is still best pursued in as much solitude as you can stand.

10. Lingua franca

While I don't have any statistics, fishing must be responsible for more cross-generational, cross-occupational,
cross-societal, cross-geographical, and cross-just-about-any-
boundary-you-can-mention *friendships* than any activity
you can compare against it. Golfers tend to golf with people
from the same office; bowlers bowl with people from the
same plant, but fishing friendships seem to flourish amid
what would seem the unlikeliest of dissimilarities, and
there's no better tribute to the richness of our sport. What
I've been struck with time and time again is how two very
different people, united by this one passion, can begin talking in a common language from the first sentence of their
conversation, exchanging secrets, trading battle stories,
instantly getting to a stage of intimacy that would take
many hours if not for this key. I don't speak French, yet I
still feel certain that if I were plopped down next to one of
those patient Seine fishermen I could have a pretty good
conversation going inside of minutes, even if it was
exchanged solely with our hands.

Add fishing partnerships to this entry, those happy com-
binations when to the instant communication of the above
is added long shared experiences on rivers and ponds. For
many fishermen it will come first in the fishing motives, and
should I ever come back to revise this list, I would hope —
if present trends continue, if people continue to ignore my
foibles and invite me out — that it would be first on mine.

11. Retribution

There can't be many activities where sins of commission
and omission are punished as instantly and inevitably as in

fishing. A hasty knot in a leader will surely find a trout to snap it; an unsharpened hook will find a bass's jaw too hard to penetrate; a clumsy step in a deep pool and over our heads we go. I am just enough of a Puritan to find this comforting; again, it goes against the grain of our century, where the wages of sin are higher than the rewards of virtue. Keenness of attention, discipline of method, fussiness over details — these are dull attributes to list, but every good fisherman has them, so there you are.

The only thing better than being a Puritan, of course, is being a lapsed Puritan — to not give a damn about knots or imitation or prudence, and just chuck the fly out there. Make that number eleven and a half on the list — a halfway step to:

12. Chance

The throw of the dice, the spin of the wheel, the play of a card — fly-fishing is as chancy as one of these, and gambling is unquestionably one of its delights, and goes far to explain the compulsive ardor many fishermen bring to its pursuit. To anyone who's made the high-wire gamble of a writing life, any lesser chance, by a cautious backlash, seems unbearably risky, and I've never been one for football pools or raffle tickets or bingo. Still, when I go out on a river I like the fact so many chances are taken — taken in big ways when the wading gets dicey or a thunderstorm brews up; taken in lesser ways almost continually: the chance there may be a trout lying in that riffle where none has ever lay before; the chance he might be in the mood for a Blue Winged Olive; the chance we can land him if we pare down to a 7X leader with a breaking strength of less than a pound. The best fisherman I know giggles a lot when he fishes —

giggles, I suspect, at so many of his risks coming off. We all
do this at some level — laugh at our good luck, curse at our
bad, so that a day on the water is a kind of catharsis, and I
often come back home at night with a throat scratchy and
sore from sheer exclamation.

13. *Hope*

Mountain climbing has been described as "the alternation
of hope and despair," and while fly-fishers in the ordinary
course of their game do not risk rockfall or avalanche, this
definition still goes a long way to explain the intensity of the
fishing passion. Despair — well, there's plenty of that, even
on a good day. Small tangles become monstrous backlashes;
leaders snap from the clumsiness of our knots; trout are rising to a hatch that is unmatchable, until we're locked out by
our ineptitude from the moment when nature exhibits itself
at its very richest.

But even that maddening, unmatchable hatch fulfills one
of the hopes we bring to the river in the first place: to see it
at the peak of vibrant life. Hope is the one prerequisite in
angling, the best part of the sport, and, I'd like to think, the
coda that has underlined this book all along. In a century
where hope has pretty well had its face smashed in, even to
wear the small hope of a fisherman is in its way a victory —
to hope for anything at all. And further — where in this age
can even small hopes be satisfied as readily and innocently
as in fishing? Estranged from nature, what other portion of
it responds even occasionally to our coaxing?

Coming to the end of *Walden* Thoreau summed up his
experiment in living thus: "That if one advances confidently
in the direction of his dreams . . . he will meet with a success unexpected in common hours." This was written from

an optimism that seems amazing to us now, and yet there are people who every day learn the truth of this, and among them are fishermen, who, in their precious hours on the water, possess an optimism and strength of purpose worthy of Thoreau. Try it the next time you go out on your favorite river. See how the four-count rhythm of fly casting synchronizes itself to the surge of hope welling up in your chest.

 I . . . fly off the water . . . *real-ly* . . . line uncoiling back of us . . . *HOPE* . . . line shooting forward.

 I . . . *real-ly* . . . *HOPE.*

That the twelve-inch rainbow there ahead of me sees the Spent Wing Adams floating down past his sheltering log.

 I . . . *real-ly* . . . *HOPE.*

That the rain lets up. That the wind doesn't collapse this cast around my head. That the Hendrickson hatch starts at two o'clock on schedule.

 I . . . *real-ly* . . . *HOPE.*

That my daughter and son will learn to love fly-fishing. That I introduce them to it with the right measure of gentle patience. That they find in it what I have found and more. That they remember to take their old man out with them when the passion takes hold.

 I . . . *real-ly* . . . *HOPE.*

That they decide not to build a freeway across the river. That the state institutes a catch-and-release stretch before the trout disappear. That the coal plants cap off their emissions and reduce acid rain. That the farmers stay in business. That flood plains are not built on or developed.

 I . . . *real-ly* . . . *HOPE.*

That trout streams run pure and wild forever. That trout and bass and every fish that swims flourishes mightily in the coming century. That man calls a truce with nature, starts the long patient healing and rejoining the lack of which dooms us all. That in the future even to talk about a separation this way will seem an ungrammatical impossibility. That the lion of man lies down with the lamb of nature, not in an allegory, but in a new realistic symbiosis.

I . . . real-ly . . . HOPE.

Add your own here — add the minor and major hopes that go into the fishing passion and so unite us once and for all. "Our tradition," wrote Roderick Haig-Brown, "is that of the first man who sneaked away to the creek when the tribe did not really need a fish, a tradition developed for us through thousands of years and millions of river lovers. We fish for pleasure, and fishing becomes pleasure from within ourselves in proportion to the skill and knowledge, to the imagination and flexibility of soul, that we bring to it." This is correctly and splendidly said, and the only thing left to do in finishing is to wish you all the best fishing in the world — wish, as intently as it's possible to wish something off the page, that once in your life the fates conspire in your favor, the planets pause in their circling, the waters part, and there beneath your uncoiling line will rise something miraculous, something worth all your longing, something extraordinarily *fine*.